Chosen
to Forgive

By

Marcus Weaver & Rick E. Roberts

CHOSEN TO FORGIVE
Copyright © 2017 by Marcus Weaver and Rick E. Roberts

ISBN 978-0-998-0882-0-4

Publisher: Chosen to Forgive
Email: chosentoforgive@gmail.com
Phone: (720) 774-4677
PO Box 2243
Arvada, Co 80001-2243 USA

Bible quotes are from:
New American Standard Bible (NASB)
Copyright © 1960, 1962, 1963, 1968, 1971, 1972, 1973, 1975, 1977, 1995 by the Lockman Foundation

New International Version (NIV)
Holy Bible, New International Version®, NIV® Copyright ©1973, 1978, 1984, 2011 by Biblica, Inc.®
Used by permission. All rights reserved worldwide.

16 Books by Rick E. Roberts   Year Published

My First Thirty Years	1995
88 Keys To Life	1997
Before Africa	1998
L'Ecrivain (the writer)	1999
Starting At The Finish Line	2000
My Tears Have Been My Food	2001
At Ground Zero	2002
Crumbs For The Little Puppies	2003
153 FISH	2004
Come And See	2005
The Remnant: Dream Another Dream	2006
Follow Me	2007
The Dreamer and The Dream	2009
Exclusively His	2014
I'll Be Your Father	2017
Chosen To Forgive	2016

            (co-written with Marcus Weaver)

Recommended Movies and Books to Help You

Good Will Hunting
The Peaceful Warrior
Antwone Fischer
A Snoodles Tale
Blindside
Chicken Soup for The Soul series

Dedication

This book is dedicated to Samuel Roberts, my son! He is an amazing man, coming of age in a world that is so different from the one I grew up in. He navigates it pretty well. He has overcome a lot and he has a gigantic heart of love. He defends the weak and he makes the lonely feel welcome. He is a loyal and kind soul and an excellent friend! I see a wisdom beyond his years and a joy that's powerful and good. He knows who he is: a beloved son, a mighty warrior, a brilliant mind, a tremendous athlete. He will succeed in whatever he chooses to do and be a light and a help to others. I am so proud of him and I love him completely, even when he calls me fat! He was my gift from Our Father to make my life complete, have purpose and redeem my greatest agony into joy.

I'm excited for who he is and who he is becoming - a priceless treasure like all of my sons. It's a parent's greatest victory to see them experience and do all that they are made for while loving the process. Here's your gold star buddy to make up for the one in 5th grade! I am glad you're my son and I'm proud of you! You belong to me and I belong to you! Just as it was supposed to be! Thank you God for making a way for us, now about that Shelby Mustang…..

Rick E. Roberts

Acknowledgements by Rick E. Roberts

I would like to thank Papa God for giving me life, for being right there when I was conceived, seeing purpose and goodness in me. You are a good Father, the only Mighty God and my friend. I bless you and I love making sunrises with you! It needs more red and gold! Just kidding. Maybe.

I would like to tell my Jesus how fun He is and how much I love Him. He is a wonderful lover of my heart, protector, teacher and friend. He is kind and silly and He loves me for who I am. I love you Jesus! Thank you for coming to find me and never letting me go!

Thank you Holy Spirit for making me a better person. I have needed your wisdom, training and laughter to get me where I am now. I have made up for lost time and grown more than I ever thought I could with your great tutelage and mentoring. I bless you and thank you. I love all you've done to make me more and I love you! Thanks for laughing with me, but try to cut down on the laughing at me please!

Thank you to my wife Melissa for being a rock in my life, for raising up amazing kids and sharing the joy of this life with me. We have done it all and there is so much more I want to do with you! Thanks for the adventure! Best thing I ever did.

Thanks to my other sons, David, Michael, Jesse and Luke. You are mighty men and I couldn't be more proud of you! I have loved watching you grow and sharing what it is to be a man. You make me better as a man and a father and I learn so much from you all. None of you came from my body, but you were born in my heart long ago. I hope I can live up to that look I see in your eyes! I bless you and I honor you! Go forth and be mighty!

To my bible study friends who have loved me and learned from me, taught me and walked with me. Thank you Boulder Men's Group, John Bandimere's group, the Men of Yeshua and Narrowgate.

To my sister, Colleen, thank you for saving me from Mom; if it wasn't for you, I wouldn't be here. For the LaBate and Kenkel family for welcoming me like one of you and helping me find my way. To Dr. King for helping me see what's important and being willing to die to get us there.

And to Graham Cooke, the best father an orphan ever had!

Acknowledgements by Marcus Weaver

First and foremost, I dedicate this book to the Lord, who makes all things possible and bears with me in times of the storm. He had mercy on my life countless times, showing me what forgiveness really is, the power of grace, and for surrounding me with the most amazing people in this world that make my time here worth living.

To my beautiful wife, Megan, who exceeds my expectations in everything she does and especially her unconditional love in and through me, her beauty and for far surpassing what I thought any relationship could be, especially a marriage . Thank you for being who you are, my eternal partner and best friend. *I LOVE YOU* Mrs. Weaver and our children; Magdelyn, Zion, Jamin, Mitchell and Jordan who all made me want to be a good father and a real dad. They have inspired me to be a better person and a better man.

To my Mom and my sisters, Zhalih and Yasmine, who saw a diamond when everyone else saw coal and loved me through the pain, the struggle and into the glory. To my entire St. Louis family, Virginia/Colorado extended family and friends spread across the country – we are here now, let's move forward and step into our blessings as a big, diverse family.

For all the people from my childhood including mentors, colleagues, co-workers and friends mentioned in this book or not, who were with me along the journey. People like Dr. Elaine Smith, Dr. Bob and Miss Eddie Woolfolk, Bo Matthews, Stan Jacobson, George Medley, Craig Redd, Greg Wade, Tammie Carroll and so many more. All those who knew me at my best/worse and are still a huge part in the road ahead. But especially to Rick Roberts whose Christ-centered friendship has helped me dream the impossible and showed me agape love when I couldn't even love myself.

To Rebecca Wingo and the twelve others whose lives were taken in the early hours of July 20, 2012 in the Aurora Theater shooting and to the thousands around the world who have had their lives cut short by senseless violence. This book is dedicated to each of you and your families. I hope these pages bring some comfort, knowing that you're not alone.

To anyone who has been hurt, abused, left behind or told they weren't good enough, may this book light the way for you into freedom and restoration.

Table of Contents

Introduction

Who Will Cry 6-21-04 by Rick E. Roberts

Who will cry for the little boy, lost, alone and afraid?
Who will cry for the old man and the decisions that he made?
Who will cry for the young man, his whole life there before him?
Who will cry for the old man as his eyes are growing dim?
Who will cry for the little boy with no daddy of his own?
Will he be a daddy, too, in years when he has grown?
Who will cry with that man, when he longs to talk to his dad?
Who will cry with that man when his memories make him sad?
Who will cry for the little boy looking up into daddy's face?
The only dad he will ever need is with him, full of grace.

My earliest memory is waking up in the night. I was maybe four years old. In my sleepiness I heard my mom crying, then some yelling, then a slap. The slap of no return. My life would never be the same again. My parents spent a lot of time drinking, fighting and never dealing with the issues from their youth. By the time I was seven they had divorced and my dad's presence in my life was severed forever. It became a source of constant anger, sadness and angst in my life. My mother and many, many step fathers became increasingly violent and she had checked out totally by the time I was ten. There was a lot of insanity during those years and I was left alone to figure life out for myself. When you're driven by heartbreak, fear and loss at an early age, a lot of crazy things can happen along the way. My name is Rick and that's part of my story.

I was an unplanned child. My mother spared my life, but things were a mess from day one. Abortion was illegal in the early 1970s, but some people ran abortion clinics out of the house and dealt secretly with many who wanted to kill their children and hide their mistake. That could have been me. My mom conceived a child with a man who

11

was already engaged to marry another lady who was also pregnant with his child, too. My biological father couldn't deal with it without admitting his guilt. That was a recipe for abortion. Hide the mess, kill the blob of tissue and cover up the act. It happens way too much. For some reason I was spared.

A ruthless and sadistic step father, an out of touch mom and many years of abuse and sorrow were in my future. I had to survive, but I felt like everyone was letting me down. Little kids need to be safe, so even if you have to spend all your time at a friend's house or elsewhere, you do what you have to do. I was the oldest, but no matter what I did, I was always made the problem. The bad son, the trouble maker. That was not me, but it's a label I carried for a long time and that can cause crazy things to happen along the way. I carried my at-risk behavior from childhood to adulthood. Life was difficult to navigate. Like a bag of rocks, pebbles and mortar way too heavy for me to carry alone. My name is Marcus and that's part of my story.

There were also good people along the way who made a difference and made some impact for good, but those years of abuse and neglect took their toll on us in many ways. It was never easy and even to this day it's still not easy. We have overcome and we believe that we have a purpose for our lives. Nothing can stop that purpose unless we allow our circumstances to overwhelm us and make us choose the victim road and stay there. We both did just that for many years, a lot of drugs, sex, crime and sorrow under the bridge for a long time, but thankfully we didn't stay there.

No one has to if they don't want to. It may take time, energy and commitment to grow up, persevere and overcome, but it's worth it. Getting free is the best battle you'll fight and the best choice you will ever make. We guarantee it! Staying free is even more important and it will take tenacity and intentionality to carry you through to a place of victory. Two battles to win and you will, if you stay in the fight, get help, build relationships and don't give up!

Our stories will be intermingled some as we go, you may not be sure who is who at times, but the stories are real and they will help you learn, grow and gain wisdom and hope. We walked separate paths in different parts of the country with different economic and social circumstances, yet our roads were very similar. We both thought about it. What makes you get to the point where you want to cut your father's throat? Is it the beatings, the violence, the silence? Is it wondering why you're treated differently than everyone else? What is happening inside him that makes it impossible for him to connect with you? So many families are being torn to shreds by this and it's only getting worse. Welcome to our world.

Most couples don't even want to be married anymore. It's okay to be friends first and maybe more later on. It is okay to wait and not give your heart away to every stranger like it's a piece of candy. I felt like a thief at times stealing from women something very precious. Seems like hardly anybody is saying this anymore. TV doesn't say it, nor the internet, talk shows, the fashions, Hollywood or the politicians. Sometimes it feels like nobody cares about helping young people make better choices or at least telling them there is another option. Of course we both have done rotten things and made a mess of our sexuality and purity, but that doesn't mean it was right or helpful in our lives.

I know first-hand, and have two children out of wedlock and both have been challenging relationships for years. Partly it was the seeds planted inside me, and partly the example from the culture around me. Even after I committed myself to wait, I remembered that the flesh is powerful. Sex can be like a drug in the culture I grew up in. Just like my Fathers before me, the competition to be the stud of the farm was intense. Everybody wanted to be the king. What's wrong with not having sex right away and waiting until you're married or at least committed to stay together?

Friends First (www.friendsfirst.org) is a great organization in Denver that offers a variety of programs through classroom presentations and workshops which are helpful for health, family, after school programs and more. I have spoken on their behalf to groups and classes for years. They are making a difference for purity. We know that's not very popular right now, but it's a needed thing and most of us would agree with that statement.

My life was almost ended because of poor choices with sexual activity. There are over fifty million babies who have had the same fate that I could have. That is a sorry legacy to leave behind! Maybe instead of that way, we could try letting babies live when we make a mistake. Why do they have to pay for our bad choices? I have five sons and they're all adopted. I think a lot of couples would love the chance to adopt a child. It's not always an easy road, but being a parent never is. It will bring out the best and the worst about you, sometimes in the same day. Try being a parent when the only example you were given was one of fury, poor choices, low morals, checking out, running around, being irresponsible and never growing up. Then it's even harder. The choice is yours to make. Everything happens for a reason. Every choice has a consequence, good or bad.

.

Chapter 1 – Batman
Marcus

Batman is one of my favorite heroes. I think I relate to him, you know. He's a fictional billionaire whose parents were murdered right in front of him as a child. He then swore an oath of revenge on criminals everywhere as a result. He is the only superhero with no "super" powers. He's a man just like anyone else and he has to rely on his wits, training, technology and strength to defeat the enemies.

I always think of him as a black man trying to get revenge for the place of dishonor given him in this world. We have had the same orphan spirit thrust upon us in so many ways. A fatherless culture and second class status is our reward. What did we do to deserve that? My great, great grandmother was a slave and was molested by the slave owner. She did nothing wrong, but she was an easy target. Are we still easy targets today? Being in the Aurora Theater shooting and having bullets whizzing by my head and into my body was something new. But in a lot of ways it felt like a continuation of what I had been experiencing my whole life. So like Batman, I had to rely on my wits, strength and talents just to survive. To defeat the enemies that came against me I needed skill and courage, and I would have to do it without having a father.

I was born at St. Luke's hospital in St. Louis and it's no longer there. St. Louis is a strange town, full of bad juju. It's like everybody is related to each other. The normal scene is people going to church or work and looking good on the outside, but not really following any good moral standards. Hypocrisy at its finest. It's a marriage on paper, but still living the party lifestyle. It's still very segregated and full of people saying "give me a check." There is so much potential there. There are so many changes that could happen there but they never seem to. It's a weird thing and I want to change it.

My Mom had met my birth father through my uncle. He was handsome, suave, and debonair. Yes, my birthfather Anthony Hill was kind of a charmer, like me. The apple doesn't fall too far from the tree. He was a light skinned Romeo with green eyes and a winning smile. His family owned several dry cleaners and he was even trying to be a professional bowler. A true All-American boy! I didn't know he existed until I was thirteen. My mom was a straight A student and was generally home caring for her younger brothers and sisters much of the time since her mom was kind of a wild lady.

She and my grandparents are the ones who started all this crazy ass behavior. Grandma really liked to go out to the clubs to go dancing. There was weed, sex and alcohol in abundance. It still is at many family reunions to this day. She was married to Doc. He secretly performed abortions on the side and made a lot of money. He made your problems go away. Sometimes I'd go over there and visit and we would go down in the basement and play pool. It was a big house and in the downstairs refrigerator would be fetuses. The smell was terrible. It's a regular practice at hospitals I guess. But in your *house*? What a strange world to grow up in.

My mom would still visit Doc even after she was kicked out for not getting an abortion. It was like he was some kind of role model or had some draw for her that she couldn't leave behind. Maybe she was searching for affirmation or a connection to the money. She didn't have a healthy sense of family. Mom's real dad was from Tennessee and she never really knew him – a recurring theme in so many lives. So many black lives especially. Her grandparents had grown up around slavery and it was still a part of the cultural backstory. Mom was stuck at home a lot, which meant she had little time for socializing and maybe she was angry about that like most young women probably would be. I never really blamed her for getting swept off her feet by a charmer. He was a player and she should have seen through him, but maybe she was lonely. Maybe he was too cute to pass up. Whatever it was, I'm glad she let me live. The legacy that all these parents and grandparents left behind for us by their wild living and choices is coming home to roost. Is that why our country is a mess right now?

My mom was pretty and one day a well-built man saw her at the bus stop and swept her off her feet again. He was a dark skin and she was a light skinned princess. He wanted her. She was the ultimate prize. Unless you are a black person, you may not understand the black inner racism that exists. First of all many of us hate white people, to be very honest. We may not know any or have any experience with them, but we hate them nevertheless. They treated us wrong, even if it was generations ago. The grudge is alive and well, fair or not. In black inner racism, the key is getting lighter. If you're a dark skinned guy you don't always marry a dark skinned girl, you look for the lighter skinned princess. It seems like we want to get lighter as we go. The lighter you are, the better you are. Somehow that is valuable to us. I don't know why. I find it ironic that we want to become what we hate. It's more complex than people realize. I have Native American and White in my bloodline, so I am milk chocolate not dark chocolate. That's a benefit in the African American culture, though many would never admit it. I think we all are mixed to some degree and at some point we all will be.

Herb was a dark skin and he saw my (Marcus') mom as his almost white princess. What better way to get back at the white man than to take his daughter and make her your own? It's sweet payback for us to get a white girl, especially if she is rich. Every time you have sex with her it's a chance to punish the white man for making us suffer under his hands. For every time he took our moms or grand mamas and made them have sex with him. For every time he inflicted pain or suffering on us. Screw him and now screw his daughter! She will love us forever and birth us beautiful light skinned children and we win! That's our mindset even to this day. Isn't it?

Inter-racial couples are common now, but in 1967 on an episode of Star Trek, Captain Kirk and Lieutenant Uhura kissed and it was almost World War 3. She was the first prime time black TV star and now they were taking our black girl? What the heck is going on? Was she a trophy to be taken? Our African Princess given over to the white master all over again? Many blacks never recovered from that slight. Maybe it got blown out of proportion, but I can see why they felt that way. 1967 was the year interracial marriage finally became legal in America. It became legal to racially intermarry in Alabama in 2000. That's a long way from 1864. It's progress, but very slow progress. Are we still uncomfortable in our own skin?

17

Mom had to leave the family when she had me. Her mom wanted her to have an abortion. Doc could do it in the basement, but she didn't want that. She had a lot of courage, she took a stand. In that culture and that time in our history, it cost her something. It gained me everything, *thanks Mom!* I remember seeing Tim Tebow in a commercial and it made me think. He could have been aborted for a supposed birth defect. I could have been aborted for a lifestyle choice. Both of our moms chose to give us life and we're glad. Tim has done some really good things. Not everyone loves him, but he has made a difference. He built a hospital in the Philippines. I hope I have done some good things, and I want to do more. Mom's Aunt Geraldine, a paragon of virtue and love, took us in while mom went to school and had me. She is a wonderful lady of 94 now. She just recently gave up bowling due to her bad knees, but she is a house of love and one of the reasons I survived and became anything at all. I went to her funeral in October while this was being edited and I miss her every day.

Back to the bus stop. Mom was already a mother and had me with her, but he liked what he saw. She did, too, especially the new car. The rest of the family was skeptical of Herbert Weaver. There was something off about this guy and they all saw it, except for my mom. She should have seen through him. They got married quickly since the no support vibe was so heavy and the promise of a brighter financial future was great. It turns out he was from a large family of 12 kids. They were all gang bangers and had all kinds of trouble around them all the time. They were crooks, thieves, drug dealers, sex perverts -- you name it. Whatever they wanted to do, it was all in the family. Herb Weaver eventually became my step dad and he was indeed a trouble maker. He threatened my birthfather and made him sign away his parental rights. Then he could adopt me. It turns out he had already been married before and had three kids with her before she went crazy, literally. I would soon understand why. Herb's parents were super strict. There was incest and violence in the family. There were suicides, sexual abuse and cruelty. That's the environment he came from and shared it all with us freely and completely.

He was a guilty criminal and found his way into a courtroom and was sentenced to a long jail term. Then the judge made him an offer he couldn't refuse. Join the service and go to Vietnam and fight in the war or go away for a long time. What a deal! He was now in the U.S. Marines. Uncle Sam, Mom, apple pie, fight for my country and let me at those communists! That's a long way from the projects and running the streets or prison! It turns out he saved a buddy over there during combat and his buddy's dad was a big wig executive at General Motors. Just like that my stepdad went from prison bound gang banger to corporate executive track. He was in the right place at the right time twice! He got out of the Marines and he had a great job waiting for him. He worked in the GM finance division after he took some accounting classes. This was an amazing job in the early 1970s for anyone, black or white.

Against the family's wishes, my mom married Herb Weaver and most of the family hated his guts. I was now a Weaver, too, not a Simmons or a Hill and we were the most privileged black family around, at least on the outside. That was important to mom I think, having money, prestige and privilege. She was no slouch either, she was a supervisor at GM but she saw an opportunity and she took it. She was an enabler, but she was also an opportunist. Family was important to her, but money was, too. He earned a good salary and we were upper middle class. We seemed stable and upright, but Herbert was a monster. He had hatred and demons inside of him that came out in pure fury. He was a control freak. It started with the food that we ate. He made sure that none of us ate white bread, pork or drank soda. We couldn't have candy, caffeine, chips or things that most other kids did. He started yelling a lot. He liked to be in charge and he let you know it. You had a line to toe and if you didn't, you got an earful. Maybe his so called success was beginning to go to his head. The abuse was just starting. He ran us through our paces with school, and I even skipped kindergarten and first grade since I was so far ahead on the basics like reading and math facts.

Later on, yelling no longer fed his sadistic streak and he graduated to vicious whippings with an extension cord. He would straighten it out and use it to rip into my flesh. The marks were everywhere on my body and in my soul. He knew where the lines on my clothes would be, so no one could see the marks. I hated him the first time he hit me and it grew every time he did it again. I felt worthless and unloved. The yelling got worse. The marks got so bad at one point, I couldn't really change for gym in front of other people. I had big marks on my back and I would go in the stall or leave my t-shirt on underneath so no one could see. I was a good student and an athlete, but I was less willing to listen and do the work at school and I started acting out a lot more. That was the first sign of abuse and no one saw. No matter what I did, after he and Mom had two kids of their own, he treated me like an outcast. He was punishing me way more than what I did. It wasn't even conditional love based on performance. I think he liked to see me cry and make me feel small. Maybe it made him feel like a tough guy or something, but I started wanting to hurt him.

We lived in St. Louis until I was five, my sister Zhalih was born there. We had a lot of family around so it kept Herb in check a little bit. The tide really turned for the worse when we moved to Ossining, New York. My stepfather was a very scary person. He made you live in fear all the time and now no one was there to keep him under control. He rode the train into the big city and was in a management training program at GMAC. Mom worked at the factory, too, so I went to the babysitter. If I missed washing a dish, he would wake me up and give me a beating and I would wash it right then. Hard to wake up to that reality. It was normal for Herb.

The beatings with the extension cord were just the beginning. Then he moved on to burning me with an iron. He pressed his clothes every day for work so it was nothing for him to brand me with a new form of abuse. This one hurt my soul deeply. I was being degraded like a worthless animal or something. I felt like I was a chameleon in training. I started learning to blend in. He was unrelenting and I knew no one here in this new place. I was seven years old the first time I ran away from home.

We lived close to the Sing Sing prison and there were a lot of people who were there for horrible things. I used to see the big wall or hear the siren and wonder what is this place? It was right along the Hudson River and probably had amazing views from within it. It opened in 1826 about 30 miles north of New York City. It's a maximum security prison with almost 2000 inmates. They did executions there, too, over 600 by electric chair. The place had a weird aura around it all the time, like death was watching us and laughing. Maybe it was. The intensity of the sorrow in my life seemed to magnify near this place of pain. Prison is never a good place, no matter what they do to it. It is not meant for any of God's children. It is necessary sometimes, and it can be a place of redemption, but it's never good or nice or easy there. This would come into play later in ways I never imagined.

We had a nice white neighborhood to dwell in. We grew up around almost all whites. Herb was into the Qu'ran, the Muslim holy book, but he grew up Catholic. He was complex and twisted in his spirituality. The Qur'an seemed to feed his anger and justify his behaviors. He wanted to rule with a sword and an iron fist. I wonder what happened to him to make him the person that I knew. He had a vindictive side, too, and he made everyone live in fear and walk on eggshells. We had plenty of everything we needed materially, but it came at a price. I ask myself, why didn't someone do something about what was going on? I knew that my two younger sisters were not safe with him around. They were his biologicals, but it didn't matter. He was cruel to us all.

By this point he made a career promotion and it was the big house in a white neighborhood with a new car every year. We had financial privilege and he sent us to private Catholic school, but he hated white people, hated Jesus and everything about Christians. An interesting contradiction I always thought. He even told us white people were animals and they ate off the floor. He said they didn't wear underwear and smelled like dogs. He said you have to know that white people don't like you and he hated them deeply. His attitude was dangerous and contagious to young minds. Yet, I started to realize that they were nothing like what my stepfather portrayed them as. Most of them were pretty decent people, some were crackers and a few treated me different because I was black. It was wild to see the nuns who took no guff, but still tried to be civil most of the time contrasted with my out of control

Herb wailing away at anything that moved or challenged his iron grip. He wasn't even trying to hide his evil anymore. He loved it.

After Grandma divorced Doc she came out for a visit. Herb treated her very poorly and she didn't stay long, this was a recurring theme for years. Family would visit and family would leave abruptly. We found out later that many of females in the family were hit on by him including most of our baby-sitters, his co-workers and Mom's friends. He was grabbing breasts and trying open mouth kisses on them. Mom never wanted to believe it though, she let him go on unchecked. He had no purity, morals, self-control or commitment to being married. I hated everything he stood for. Everything he was. I still do. Where was Batman to protect me from the evil one?

Chapter 2 - Rocky Road
Rick

I love ice cream, especially rocky road. It's made with chocolate, nuts and marshmallow. To me it exemplifies the different varieties of life. The chocolate represents the smooth, sweet times that we go through in most of life. The marshmallows are the super sweet and celebratory times like your wedding day, graduation, a new baby, all the pinnacle moments. The Broncos winning the Super Bowl comes to mind. The nuts are the hard places, the rocky roads filled with danger, struggle, sorrows and regret. That's where my life began, right in the nuts. In some ways my parents needed their insanity to survive. They made a life out of chaos, drama and weirdness long before reality TV glorified it and went mainstream. Just like the T-shirt their motto was, "I don't suffer from insanity, I rather enjoy it!" That was their life and mine. Choose your vice and pay the price.

Mom stayed home with me for a while after I was born but went back to work soon after. They had just bought a new house in Cucamonga, California, about thirty miles east of Los Angeles. My dad worked at General Dynamics in Pomona as a dock man and forklift driver and he made a good living. He was a chain smoker, heavy drinker and he had this really bad habit of going to the bars after work and not coming home right away or at all. He later said, "She didn't want to go anywhere, she didn't want to have sex or travel. She never wanted to do anything." She was a bank teller and pretty good at her job. Her inability to cope with life left him somewhat alone, too. Is there more to the story?

Mom had three kids from her first marriage by the time she was 21. She was married to George when she was 17. He talked her into lying about her age, went to another state and got married without telling her parents. It wasn't a legal marriage and it wasn't a right one. They had hell to pay later. That ten mile drive to Oregon changed my family forever and not for the better. It would be jail time now, but in those days, it was just something to shrug your shoulders at and everybody moved on, especially in a small town. She was pretty and he was 22. He had a tattoo from the service and was a worldly guy in every way, charming, smiling and a good talker. He had that old west mustache that she liked in her men and he drew her in to a new life of deception, sorrow, regret and three little babies.

They divorced after a few years and then she met my dad. He had great hair. They met in the bar and they lived in the bar. They got married in Las Vegas and went to the bar to celebrate. When they got back, my sister moved in with them, but my two brothers stayed with their Dad. The separation of the siblings began and has endured for the rest of their lives. Funny how fifty years can roll on by without any resolution. If that's you, make an effort to change it today. Put down this book and fix what is missing if you can. You never know when a miracle can happen and if it's too late, please forgive yourself for not trying sooner.

So George Sr. and his new wife Isabelle were raising four boys together, each had two from a previous marriage. They were all within three years of each other in age. That must have been something to see. I hardly got to know my brothers (Mike and George). I spent some time with my brother George before he passed away in July. My sister Colleen looked out for me even though Mom moved her back and forth between the two houses and treated her like the problem.

About sixteen months after they married, my parents had me. A little boy in a perfect world. There was a nice brand new house being built to live in. Two parents who worked, plenty of food, clothes that fit, I even had my own room and so did my 9 year old sister. It's the American dream, until you see it from the inside. Then it was something very different. After mom went back to work, I remember going to various babysitters. Some were nice, some were not and that's where the sexual abuse started. They were unwilling to care for me themselves so I was sent out.

I remember a man with tan skin who was there with the lady babysitter sometimes and that's where things happened that should never ever happen to little people. I was starved for affection and I was made a target. It was sick and twisted. That's how a lot of predators are, they recognize you're hurt, abandoned or wounded, then they act like a friend, they compromise you and/or they make you afraid that you will be hurt, threaten someone you love or they will tell what you did like it's your fault. This technique is especially effective and destructive in runaways and orphans being converted in sex trafficking victims. They prey on the troubled kids first either by exploitation right away or grooming them over time.

It was perfect bondage and I would happily cut their throats if I could track them down. The rage is still fresh all these years later. Boys get abused, too. I have chosen to forgive them, but not to forget. I was at risk and I was made a victim. I won't tell you what all was done, but there was various sexual interaction between us. The fucked up part, was every Friday when I was five or so, I was given a dime so I could get a double scoop Rocky Road ice cream cone from the Thrifty Drug Store across the street. I was basically being bribed with something I loved to keep quiet. I hate the feeling of exploitation. That's why I support organizations that work to end human trafficking. No one should have to go through what I went through, ever! A really good one is Not for Sale. Check them out at (www.notforsalecampaign.org). They help rescue sex slaves and exploited workers from terror and a life of slavery. It's the fastest growing industry in the world and it's not going away anytime soon. Slavery is greater now than at any time in history and we're doing almost nothing to stop it. Understanding slavery, you would think this was the top issue for all Americans, but we're still too busy being offended.

My parents were oblivious to it all, lost in their world of alcohol, drugs and whatever else. There was a sick strangeness around my life. Wetting the bed was common, as was feeling afraid, vulnerable and worthless. I was the only kid at the babysitter's house so it was easy for them to hide the abuse and the destruction going on. It was easy for Mom to pass it off as "he is shy or just sad about his sister moving out again." She was my babysitter sometimes, my protector and my refuge. I'm so thankful for her! I was an awkward kid, the tallest in my class and very smart, but the abuse I endured was making me socially inept, awkward and emotionally immature. I could do well in school, and get along with most people. I was still in pure survival mode at that point and it didn't let up for many years. All kids struggle with the first awareness of their imperfections, but mine were multiplied like rabbits in the spring. Somedays it was hard just to breathe. It's the fight or flight mechanism active with a very high level of stress. When you are traumatized your body often goes into survival mode. It could be a real or perceived threat when you have to fight or run to survive. It's typical in a predator and prey interaction, but it's also linked to PTSD, crimes of violence like rape and incest or other traumatic events. PTSD is no joke.

My dad had this idea for building a really cool backyard paradise. He had a plan for a large pond with bridges, waterfalls, decorative lighting, tiki statues, bamboo plants, a bar in the garage and more. It was a big project. It consumed a lot of his off time and weekends, so they were home more because of it and within a year it was amazing. It was in newspapers and magazines, what a place! Life was better for a while and my parents got along more. Alcohol was still a central focus though since the bar was in the backyard. Behind us was a 160 acre orchard with apple and avocado trees. It was my refuge and I loved it there. It was a magical place for me to explore as my own backyard. There were animals in abundance, foxes, wolves, even bear paw scratches on one tree. I never saw that bear though.

The farmer that ran it was really smart. One day he saw my neighbor and me and he came over and said, "If you want to eat an apple or two while you're out here, that's fine, but don't pick what you won't eat." There was wisdom, generosity and kindness wrapped in what he said. Being six year old boys, there was a chance we might get into mischief by having wars with fruit or loading up on it to share with friends. He completely defused us before we ever became bombs to go off. He didn't say no, he said yes with a limit. He didn't say get out of here, he said, I'll share it, and I want you to look after it, too. He taught me so much in that encounter. Imagine if we all thought like that? We not only obeyed what he asked us to do, we also became the defenders of the orchard! We took ownership over it, because he brought us to a place of honor, responsibility and freedom. He called us up to be men. If he had said "stay out of here", we would have had a great challenge before us to overcome and defeat him and it would have become our all-consuming quest. Instead he made us guardians over it. There was love and responsibility in what he did. I always think about that and wish I could thank him. Lessons like that last a lifetime. He taught me more in that moment than my parents ever did.

We changed babysitters and that should have been a wonderful miracle. My mom found a new babysitter right down the street, how handy except she was a witch. No, really! A card carrying, broom riding, potion making, cauldron cooking lunatic of a woman. Out of the frying pan and into a strange new fire. She had a lot of kids she watched in the neighborhood. It was a hellhole. The kids were all sexually abused and we acted out on each other, too. There were little twisted games that we all would play. I think the witch was behind some of it, but the kids activated it, too. Putting things inside each other, making suggestive poses and touching. It all felt very natural but it wasn't. One older girl was kind of the ringleader. So this went on just a few houses away. My parents were unaware. They didn't care anyway. There was beer to drink and cigarettes to smoke. Life appeared good when reality was altered by an alcohol haze.

Most of the kids in that area were from inner city families, but we had this new perception of wealth because we got to move out of our apartments into these brand new houses. The old neighborhood was pretty diverse, a lot of Latinos, some blacks, some Asians. It's where I learned to get along with the other ethnicities and diverse people groups. We were all in the same boat of being poor, so we looked out for each other then. There was no competition really but there was a sense of community. It wasn't perfect, but it was real. That all changed when we moved into the new all white subdivision. It wasn't bad, it was new rules and expectations. A very different way of doing things and hiding things. The whiteness wasn't the problem, it was the self-sufficiency of everyone. We didn't need each other. We hid from life. We needed each other and now somehow we didn't anymore. It was a dangerous new way that brought lots of peril with it. Not knowing your neighbors was laziness, very unwise and it still is even today.

So my mom hooked up with this guy named Jerry, the brother of my witchy baby sitter. He looked like an old west gunslinger and pretty much lived the life, too. He drank hard, listened to old country albums like Marty Robbins and Frankie Layne and had a strange way of finding trouble everywhere. My parents got divorced, and we moved to another part of town. No more witch lady, but the scars lingered.

I was dying inside in constant emotional turmoil. I was a bright kid, but totally withdrawn. I was a good athlete and a good student. No one ever asked me what was wrong. I'm not sure I could have told them if they had. It was my first time away from dad. How come he didn't call or come over at all? Did he hate me, was it my fault? Kids choose to blame themselves for divorce, it's crazy and not true, but we do it. We somehow make it our fault and we believe it. After a short time, I ran away back to my old house when she wouldn't let me in one day. I was seven and I walked a long way to get there. It was seven miles and much of it on a busy main road. I almost got hit by a car. My old neighbor's drove by, recognized me and picked me up and took me to their house. It felt good to run, even if I didn't know where I was going. I got beat bad for that one. Mom had moved us out one day when dad was at work and she took everything there was, even every fork, towel and all the furniture. She left him a bed and his clothes. No soap, sheets or laundry detergent. Nothing at all. She was a spiteful woman and she knew how to inflict pain. I was learning to hate her every day.

I had the chance to skip third grade since I was far ahead, but mom said no. I was smart, why not take advantage of it? Another setback in an ocean full of bitterness. So after a year of shacking up, Jerry's company moved us to Colorado when I was nine. My real dad and I were finished forever. A thousand miles away, but it might as well as have been a million. I hardly saw my dad again after that. The worst part was, I left my sister behind, too. She always looked out for me when no one else did. She defended me against Mom more times than I can count and she took several beatings from Mom for her kindness. One day I told her these six guys were threatening to beat me up. She marched right over there, got in their faces and told them off. It was six against one and she faced them all down and they ran off. She was only a couple of years older, but her attitude and body language said it all. It was awesome! She was unafraid, unlike me.

This new relationship of Mom and Jerry, it was cat and mouse from day one. He and Mom found new ways to be stupid crazy together. It was the drinking at first, drugs and then he started going to the strip clubs. It wasn't the normal middle of the road perversion club, it was the vomit on the floor, hot and cold running gonorrhea and prostitution in the bathroom sort of place. The alcohol abuse was worse than ever and I remember one night Jerry being passed out drunk on the floor in our apartment. I don't know what he said, but after he passed out on the floor, I remember my Mom grabbed a huge glass ashtray and hit him in the temple with it. He started bleeding. I thought she had killed him. I wanted to kill him.

Another night he said something extremely rude and sexual to my sister. I went outside, kicked out a fence board with nails sticking out and I was going to kill him with it. I came back into the house to see my sister dump an entire drawer of silverware searching for a knife to stab him with. Thankfully the police came before we all ended up in prison or the morgue. That was the beginning of the end for them, thank God! It was pathetic to see how dangerous they were together. If that sounds like you, do yourself a favor and get away from the people that make you toxic or crazy. Separate is better, and necessary to survive. Seriously, don't wait. Make a plan and do it now! Your life can be better when you take a step toward healing and safety.

My Mom and he would go out to the bars almost every evening during the week and then she tried to catch up on her sleep on Saturdays. Once I made the mistake of waking her up during the catch up on her sleep time and she came flying out of her bedroom and beat the crap out of me for it. What happened to her to make her believe that that was an acceptable response to a little bit of noise? When you don't rest, it makes you irrational in many ways. She needed release from whatever the demons of her past were. Maybe guilt over lying about her age to get married. Maybe something else happened. I think she was sexually abused, too, but we never talked about it. I wonder who did it, maybe her father, maybe a husband or another guy? I don't know. I hate how she had to struggle and made us struggle with her.

One time she moved us away to Montbello. It was an all-black neighborhood in Northeast Denver, it felt like home. He found us and moved us back the same day. She amazed me though, even though she lived this vagabond life and stayed out most of the time, she always managed to go to work the next day. Mom had this bad habit of grabbing whatever was available and beating you with it when she was pissed off, which was frequently. One day she broke a hair brush over my arm and I looked at her and she knew she would never, ever touch me again. The look on my face told the story: if she did it again, I would kill her and I meant it.

The apartments were being converted to condos and one day I said, "Can we just move out of this place?" Amazingly, she agreed and the eight years of violence and strangeness with Jerry were over. Within a few weeks, I never saw him again. Being the kid of a struggling single Mom never worked out well, you instantly sank to the bottom of the economic pecking order and all the kids knew it: the days of the new house were long gone and a new reality came in. Your pants don't fit; your shoes are too tight; you wear the same clothes you had last year. Stuff is dirty or worn. It made you feel like a pariah.

Most of the kids still had two parents, but I had the step father of the week club. Mom would bring home whatever random guy from the bar. They were usually not the cream of the crop to begin with, and my life would get more complicated having to navigate new situations, risks and whatever drama they brought to this whole insanity thing around my life. Most of the time they moved right in with little or no warning. I didn't like the vulnerability of that. Especially after being sexually abused, I was always on guard and thinking, "Who is this asshole, am I going to have to kill him to survive?" It was him or me, fight or flight. Being constantly in that place of anxiety and stress wears you out and messes you up in every way.

Chapter 3 - Frederick Douglass
Marcus

We had a babysitter called Floretta who used to play around with me sexually in the bathtub and force herself on me. Looking back, it was sick; but if this is your only example of life, it's hard to understand that life could be this toxic, being abused by someone in a position of trust. She was fifteen and I was maybe seven. She would make my sister stay in her room while she did this to me so she wouldn't be detected. I wonder who taught it to her. I think that she stopped being our babysitter because my dad tried to make the moves on her. Herb didn't care if you were under age, he was a predator, plain and simple. My cousin, Shirley, came to help out with the babysitting one summer and she had to be fifteen or so. She left quickly because Herb was trying to kiss and hit on her, too. I ran away that day. I found that running helped, even if I wasn't really escaping.

Later I was pretending to be stupid in school on purpose and I got a beating each time for it. Herb would not tolerate that. I went to the Catholic school and the first day I did my multiplication tables, so obviously I wasn't stupid. Herb always wanted us to excel at school, it was the one benefit of his tyranny and control. Unfortunately, he squandered the great opportunities he had. He made money, but he had to play the part, do the song and dance for the white men above him at GM. That's what it seemed like. The pressure was on and it made him furious with no end! Like a puppet to the master. His fury was fueled daily.

Later on my grandmother came out to see us and Herb didn't like her being around because he felt that she was trying to disrupt his world. Everybody was on to him. If anybody ever came to visit us he treated them so bad that they would want to leave right away. Even my mom's friends would tell her that "Herb hit on my daughter while she was babysitting your kids." Mom still didn't listen. Herb thought he was God's gift to women because of the money and the power. Men get messed up in the head when they have money. They think they deserve everything: women, drugs, alcohol and whatever!

31

It's pride. Guys go on power trips when they have cash. He was a high achiever for that time in the black culture and it messed him up. I remember seeing rolled up hundred dollar bills in the washing machine long before I ever knew what cocaine was. He was a hard worker, but he never addressed those demons inside and they were getting bigger and stronger than he was; that can be true for any of us. His family was in abject poverty, so having the money went to Herb's head. Never having any money before can mess you up if you're not careful. Growing up a gun-toting gangster and walking into the executive suite was a hard adjustment for him. It was lethal. He found a new mindset of anything goes. He thought he was entitled to anything he wanted and he went after it with all he had. He wanted and demanded everything his way. He beat me one time for eating a non-beef hot dog at my friend's house. He wanted everything confidential and quiet around our house and at school, that's the kind of guy he was. He could sneak attack that way. If everyone knew he was a predator, he couldn't keep being one. Is this what happens to men when they start believing that everyone else is beneath them? Or when kids who grow up in tremendous sorrow and poverty get an opportunity and can't handle it. The hard part is how that is passed on to the next generation, which was me.

We never knew if he was happy, sad or furious and the stress of never knowing which Herb would show up, was crushing. He was mean and vicious now in his pursuit to control everything, even our emotions. We had all the latest cool things, great clothes, even the first VCR in our neighborhood. We had it all, including PTSD, insanity, depression and deep hatred toward him. I was so busy processing the abuse, I couldn't think or dream at home. I was also doing stupid things trying to find my identity and was willing to be mediocre to fit in. The rich black family was so dysfunctional, we set new standards daily. I still could keep it together at school pretty well. I understand that we're under different rules now but for a long time I could be funny, even distracting and get away with it. It felt like I was a double agent, you never tell on your family in the African-American community. It started me getting in trouble more, all the processing I had to do. The sorrow, the pain, the anger, it was intense. Even if you're a good student, teachers won't tolerate you disrupting their class for long! Part of my acting out was being bored and not knowing what to do with the pile of crap that was my life. He would beat us horribly behind my mom's back and then take us to McDonalds to try to make us feel better. Who does that?

About the same time, I was being inspired by a twelve part TV series, "Eye on the Prize" all about Dr. Martin Luther King Jr.'s life and the civil rights movement. Also the TV miniseries, "Roots," which talked about slavery in a real and powerful way. It mobilized me to stand up for my race and celebrate Dr. King. I always wanted to emulate him because he was willing to take a stand for us. Are we still today? He put his money where his mouth was and even died to help us come forward into a new reality. It's territory we are still fighting for even today. It wasn't just about our race though, it was about justice for common and poor people, even the White, Asian and Latino ones. Sometimes we forget that, it's not just about only our race. Dr. King loved the poor and wanted justice for all, for everyone, even the white people. Being poor and put out was redefined by his bravery. A whole culture changed because he was firm in his convictions and mighty in his deeds. Freedom rarely comes any other way. Our country is filled with many situations that need our attention like this did. I cannot wait to take them on and win. Black lives are important, but poverty, abuse and neglect know no color. It's time for us ALL to rise up. Let's be unified and inclusive so we can fix this mess.

Dr. King told us: don't drink from the cup of bitterness. Right now, we in the black community are recycling our hatred, our poor treatment and our mistrust of white people and the police. Most of us are carrying someone else's racial hate crimes and offenses in addition to our own. We all have some experience of these things and there is no effort here to downplay it. We have, unfortunately, allowed these things to fester and take root deeply in every part of our spirits. There is a need to deal with these issues, but maybe the first step is to offer forgiveness to the offenders, to look at our own hearts and see what's there that's keeping us in chains still. Does that seem like a big leap? It may not change them or their hearts, but it will change us as a people. We will free ourselves from the baggage of the past that has for so long been a source of death for us and everyone in our culture. The Civil War is over, but much work remains to be done to set all the captives free completely. This may be the most important step we can take right now. I was uncomfortable with myself and it had very little to do with race. It had everything to do with how I was treated. Let's focus on that and not borrow someone else's suffering or struggle, let's not live in the bitterness of life and give up trying to make it better. There is a whole generation dealing with the troubles being passed onto them like so much bad DNA. Forgiveness is the antidote we need. That unity must come forth or we will destroy ourselves from within.

For too long, we had to endure our place of sorrow and slavery and now we can come forth in a different way. We must be speaking and acting from a place of freedom not a place of victimization, anger or hatred. The nations are raging around us and it's time for all the sons and daughters to come forth into victory. It's time to be what we really are, not what the culture, history or the media is telling us that we are. "Our inheritance from this day forward is not sorrow, or shame or fury. It is life and hope and joy, free on the inside," Dr. King said. But this doesn't happen unless we engage with it. Free on the inside will not happen unless we change our approach. The white people will not do it for us. Neither will anyone else.

This is not just true for blacks, but for the Native Americans, Japanese, Vietnamese, Women, Muslims and so many other groups. America is not perfect, but we have some reconciliation to do. It's not just the blacks who were treated poorly. I think it's important we remember that, it's not just us. I saw a clip of Michael Brown's uncle forgiving the Ferguson Police and it did something in me. That's the kind of leadership we need going forth. How can we share what we feel? We have to be honest about it. But we have to be careful not to stay there and build our own prison within the wounds. If we do that, we're even worse off than we were. There is no doubt that black people have been historically treated poorly in America. I hate to say it, but some of that is our fault. We don't promote family, we don't sacrifice to send our kids to college, we often take the easy way out and have abortions at record rates. Two-thirds of black babies are born out of wedlock. We are hurting

34

our own cause. If we are more just in how we treat each other, maybe others would treat us better. It's high time we start acting like the great people we are and not the gangsters, players, thugs, charmers and rebels that we portray. We've been sold an image, but that is not who we are. We need to change it or it's our fault.

Frederick Douglas was a man of action. After escaping slavery by jumping a train in 1838 and pretending to be a free sailor, he became a leader in the abolitionist movement. It was less than 24 hours to freedom for him. He said, "I felt as if I had escaped from a den of hungry lions, there was joy that no words could describe." He became a licensed preacher in 1839 and refined his oration skills. William Lloyd Garrison was a white man who wrote a weekly journal against slavery called the Liberator and had a great influence on Douglass. When Douglas was criticized for dialoguing with slave owners his response was, "I would unite with anybody to do right and with nobody to do wrong."

Let's do that. We can't just point out the flaws in our world. We have to be willing to get to know those who are opposed to us and see what's really going on with them. If we just point fingers and call down judgement and scorn, we will miss the opportunity to learn and grow and educate the slave owners, too. Maybe someone hurt them and maybe we have a chance to help them get to a place of freedom. Maybe it's not just about us. Politics in our day is filled with this need. Let's at least consider the possibility. Douglass was not just against slavery, he helped champion women's rights, including to the right to vote, public education, abolishing capital punishment and temperance. He was Native American, African and European descent. Douglass used the idea of the Golden Rule as a reason against slavery. Treat others as you wish to be treated. In a letter to his former slave owner Thomas Auld he said: "How would you like it if I did to your daughter Amanda, what you did to me and my family? Your wickedness and cruelty committed in this respect on your fellow creatures are greater than all the stripes you have laid upon my back or theirs. It is an outrage upon the soul, a war upon the immortal spirit, and one for which you must give account to our common Father and Creator."

"Knowledge is the pathway from slavery to freedom," Douglas said. Why are we still lagging so far behind in education when it is the way out for us? We're not all going to be Beyonce' or Michael Jordan. We have to be smart about what we do with our time, maybe we can pursue improving our lives more than hanging out at the club. If our lives matter, it's up to us to change them for the better. That's going to take work, commitment and leaving the past behind. We can't act immorally and expect life to change. We can't act like fools and wonder why our lives are hard. Jackie Robinson had a tremendous load to bear and he did it. Not just for himself, but for every one of us. People he didn't know and would never meet. He didn't do that so we could stay on welfare and bitch and moan. He did it so we could be more, much more! These victories are hard fought and we need to keep them and keep going for it with all that we've got! He said, "A life is not important except in the impact it has on other lives." Well said Jackie, well said. Who are you helping?

Chapter 4 - Snow Day
Rick

So I came to Colorado when I was nine. The first night we had to break into our rental house because no one was around to let us in. We spent the first night on the floor after driving through snow in the mountains. You've never seen hairpin curves until you've driven through Berthoud Pass with a thirty foot horse trailer with all your possessions on it. I came outside the next morning and I moved the plastic sheathing protecting our stuff and a cascade of cold water hit my face with a vengeance. That was my first day in Colorado. I remember looking up at the sky and asking, "What am I here for?" The question is still being answered today.

I have a friend Mike and he was the first friend I met when we moved to Colorado. His family was a lot like mine: second husband with mom, one boy and one girl. It was a great place of escape for me. They were close to what I think a normal family could be. We had our issues, but it was so much more pleasant to be there than at home. I started spending the night on Fridays and sometimes I would stay the whole weekend. They had a nice house with a big yard, dogs and trees. They were wonderfully supportive of me and I was grateful for them. I think they knew what I was going through at some level and had compassion for me. Jean, Mike's mom, was a really good cook and she got a kick out of making me piles of food and watching my glee over eating it all. (She still does many years later!)

I did not know at first that Mark, the step dad, was an outlaw motorcycle club member and it was very organized. There was stolen merchandise in the garage. There were drugs of all kinds available. We had pot, crank, cocaine, mushrooms, alcohol, pornography you name it. It was a sickening scene, but in some ways I loved it. I found the medication to treat my wounded soul. Even in this horrifying scenario, I found a version of life. There were people who cared about me. Maybe it was messed up, but at least we had each other's back. That is one thing that makes gangs so popular. There is a sense of family and loyalty. You don't get that when your family kicks your ass every day.

But as it happens, it did nothing for the wounds I had, it just added more junk to my pile. So we played pinball and pong, got wasted and played sports, too. By this time, Mark's two sons had moved in and we had four of us to play and party and think up new ways to be bad. One of the things we did was go to the Northglenn Mall. The original buildings are no longer there. We were maybe 12 and we would start off at the grocery store and get a paper bag from the checkout line. Then we would go around the mall and see what merchandise was there this week. It was one of the coolest malls around and was always packed. It was the perfect cover for all that we could steal, and we did. We brought home a full bag every Saturday.

After a while we learned that if you only stole candy, you could sell that at school and make money. When you had money you could buy drugs and make more money. We had quite the little criminal enterprise going on. Surprisingly, we were not the only ones doing it, but because we kept a low profile and got good grades, nobody really seemed to care what we did. There were a lot of strange things going on in my life but the entrepreneur inside of me was starting to rise up, not in a good way, but it was there. For a kid who lived in apartments all the time, it was a step up to have cash in hand and whatever I wanted.

I remember one day it snowed a lot and school got cancelled. I was home by myself looking out the window. The snow was piling up and suddenly there was a knock at the door. I opened it to see three girls I knew from school. I let them in and I noticed they were wearing winter coats. Then they helped me notice they were wearing just underwear and bras underneath. It was a teenage boy's dream come true. The panties were so shiny and nice. One girl lived in the same building and I guess the other two came for a visit. Three beautiful girls and one hunky guy, imagine what can happen. The girls asked me to show them something and I did. So much of my identity for the next few years was tied to this event. As exciting and thrilling it was, it was also degrading and painful. We all were sexually abused and now we were acting it out on each other in a fog of lust and pain. Innocence lost unwillingly first and now pouring gasoline onto a bonfire of shame, sorrow and exploration. Wherever you are girls, I'm sorry for what happened. In my distorted reality it was a dream come true. In truth it was a massacre, a symptom of what was wrong in my life and what was wrong in my heart and I went after it with all the gusto I could manage. Three beautiful girls, what a legacy. I had a hard time looking any of them in the face later. We never talked about it and never did it again. One girl moved away shortly after, the other two within a year. It was a weird, wonderful and bitter moment. Somehow my world was made more painful that day and I felt like it was my fault. Why couldn't I have been stronger and done the right thing this time?

For me, it fueled my lust at levels that I did not know was possible. After that I wanted to be with every girl that was cute or gave me the time of day. I had finally found some confidence, but most of the girls weren't ready for or willing to have sex then. So I had to settle for less most of the time, kissing and touching. What a user I became. I was willing to grab girl's butts even in front of their boyfriends. They acted mad, but I knew they loved it. Just like me they wanted to feel like someone was paying attention to them. They pretended to be innocent, but I knew better, I knew they wanted to be seen by someone. Even if it was messed up. Some of them loved the fights that would happen over them. The battle of the studs was on for control of the harem! I started seeing the world for what it was, a place where affirmation was important, even if it was twisted wrongly. Sex was in demand and I went for it with no hesitation. I met a girl at the bus stop one day and I told her my name was Rex. She said, "Rex for sex?" Guess what happened next?

How many people in our generation were sexually taken advantage of? There is such a large group of us it's scary. Did it happen to all of our parents, too? Is that why they passed it on to us or allowed it to happen to us over and over. It's time for a whole broken and mistreated generation to face the truth. To acknowledge and accept what was done to us. Not willingly as victims and weak pieces of garbage, but with understanding. We have to face it, because no one else will do it for us. We have to get angry, be ready to feel the fury that would lead us to cut off the heads of those who did this to us. To those who afflicted us and stole our innocence. At the same time realizing this: that it also wasn't our fault. It's not my fault and it's not your fault what happened to us and that killing them will really solve nothing. In fact it would make us victims, and murderers. That doesn't fix the mess, it adds another pile to it. We have to overcome it and get past it. I'm sick of seeing so many of us going through it and now it's time for us to take back our lives, our sexuality and our authority. We don't have to like it, but if we do nothing, we allow ourselves to be permanently defeated. Instead we must defeat the single greatest obstacle in our generation. We have to forgive, not to set the guilty party free, but rather to set ourselves free. No one wants to be the victim of this, but if we don't deal with it, that is all we will be. We can't be forever defined by what happened to us and we must instead be defined by what we did to get past it. That is our challenge; the site of our greatest tragedy will also be the site of our greatest victory! We can do it and we must! We are going to offer some exercises and resources to help you later on in the book so you can do it, too. You can even help others get free as well. It's time, and you don't have to do it alone.

Chapter 5 – Men
Rick

Why do the men in ours and previous generations, ourselves included, struggle and turn away from their families in droves? It's the worst epidemic in the history of the planet. What a tragedy! How did we get here? I've thought about it long and hard and it seems like there are multiple answers. One of the biggest factors is legalized abortion. Once potential kids and sexual behaviors could be dealt with quickly, easily and discreetly, there was no reason to get married and raise a family. It took away responsibility from the equation for a few hundred dollars. So why change behavior when we can cover it up and keep doing it? It warped our sense of right and wrong and it made a whole generation of kids disappear, Marcus was almost one of them.

I've heard 58 million abortions to date and that sucks. Planned Parenthood was set up by Margaret Sanger and Ethel Bryne. Their desire was not reproductive health or education, but rather to eradicate an entire generation of "human weeds, reckless breeders, spawning…human beings who should have never been born." This quote is from Manger Sanger's book "Pivot of Civilization," referring to immigrants, African Americans and poor people. More African-Americans have died from abortion than from accidents, AIDS, violent crimes, heart disease and cancer, combined. That legacy of death is haunting us. Do you feel it? We all have free speech and free will, and those freedoms have consequences, good or bad. The choice is ours to make. I wonder what was lost in those choices. Cures for cancer and other diseases, unlimited energy inventions, amazing music, medical breakthroughs, who knows? What did we forfeit in our selfishness?

Another big factor was no fault divorce. In Russia, after the Bolshevik Revolution were the first defining decrees for no-fault divorce. It was a valuable piece of the Socialist agenda for them to eliminate marriage. The purpose of the law was ideological and to revolutionize society at every level. By removing marriage, they could weaken society as a whole and use that chaos to dominate. That happens a lot in our society today, too, by the way. In the United States, they have been pretty successful at it. Free love is the ultimate aim of a socialist state. Is that your aim, too? Look around at the mess we're in. Divorce or lack of marriage at all is a wild fire out of control. It's not utopia after all like the Socialists want you to believe. It is chaos and weakness, a perfect entry point for evil intent.

Ronald Reagan signed no-fault into law in California in 1969, first in the United States, and the divorce rate skyrocketed. Reagan even said of all the things he ever did or promoted in office, that no-fault divorce was by far the worst! No kidding! Over half of all marriages now end in divorce and so many people are afraid of it, that they just live together and never make that commitment to each other anymore for the short term benefits. Many states enacted common law marriage, which is basically an economic function. Maybe it's better than the lying charade of the past where spouses would lie about some cruel treatment to satisfy legal statutes to get out of marriage. It's really messed us up, nobody takes promises or long term commitments the same way anymore. Now it's about only what we can get, not what we can give. We have become shallow, selfish people who look to ourselves first and rarely consider others. A golden anniversary of 50 years of marriage used to be the standard to strive for, now ten years is seen as some great accomplishment. Maybe we need to get serious about what matters and start being honest and realistic, and thinking about how we can make our partner happy, not just ourselves. What a challenge ahead of us!

Another factor is this whole idea of women taking the role of leadership in the homes and things are out of balance. Women are important and to be celebrated. This is in no way to diminish them. Yet there is a usurping going on that is not healthy. Women want to be in control and men are becoming feminized and less willing to lead, provide for and protect their families. In this scenario, men are emasculated, removing their primary purpose to life and so they drift unfulfilled and uncertain in who they are. This is especially true if they are raised by women. There is no modeling of manhood, no rite of passage or acceptance as a man in the tribe and therefore their whole identity is tied up in the culture or things like clothes, sports or money; Instead of in quality of character issues like honesty, education, hard work and being a man of integrity. Those character issues that Dr. King held so dear and so indicative of where we are as a people are now hardly mentioned. I'm sorry but if you're robbing a store and something bad happens, there's a pretty good chance that it is your fault. If you are harmed when you're doing nothing at all, then that's a different story. If we want to rise as a people, we have to get back to being judged by the quality of our character first and foremost. If we start doing good things again, we will receive good things to ourselves.

Being a single mom is a horribly difficult job, and we applaud women who do it. No man or woman needs to try and control the other, but the lack of balance needs some refinement. Men need to take their role are providers, protectors, guardians and leaders and act with gentleness and respect. Women need to nurture, encourage, provide and mold children while serving their family with a kind and gentle heart. Both men and women need to be equal partners and agree on the direction of life, finances and more, but they also need to act within the role they were made for. Domestic violence is an epidemic and over 4000 women and children are beaten to death every year by a father or male partner. We need a different way. This version of family that we have now is not working. Take a look around. Men are becoming feminized and women are not needing men at all. They can be super mom, work all day and night. That's too much work for one person. It's a lot better if you have help in the home. Two parents are better for you and better for the kids. Let's turn back the clock a little.

Too much of our country is disconnected in the family units and structure. Marriage and family are the basic units of society. Without those in place, there is chaos and sorrow. Look around! It's a lot easier to take over a country when we're all disconnected, depressed or unfulfilled. When things are working right, life makes sense and there is joy in the hearts of the people, they are very strong. It's impossible to take over America, or any nation, if we're doing well. If we're depressed, without unity and everything is against us, we are easy prey and ripe for the taking. This is what a few are trying to do to us right now. If we believe the communist manifesto is the way, we are very foolish. It consolidates power into the hands of a very few and the result is Nazi Germany and the Iron Curtain all over again. We become slaves to a system with poverty and need built in, instead of a self-determining system (free enterprise) where we can make our own way. America is imperfect, but it's the best thing going on planet earth, rise up and defend it, before it's too late! Socialism promises equality, but it is a lie that will bankrupt our way of life and enslave us and our children. Reject it completely!

Chapter 6 - The Almost Cosby Family
Marcus

We were the successful black family or so it seemed. We had the big back yard and the swing set, but my parents did not really socialize with other families or Herb would sabotage the relationships. That was unique during the mid to late 1970s because house parties, disco dancing and club time were all the rage then. Dinner parties, progressive dinners and lots of socializing in the suburbs grew during those years. I think Herb was jealous of my Mom and my relationship. We were close and both lighter skinned. Maybe he somehow felt ripped off because of us being lighter. I felt ripped off because of her apathy. There were plenty of opportunities and options to get us out of that situation and she never even tried. Success made a powerful statement. She was able to get us to safety, but she chose to allow us to be destroyed because she liked the comfort of money in my view. Her parents kind of rejected her when she got pregnant and made her feel like she had to choose between them and keeping me. She got that part right. *Thanks Mom!* He was a black man making insane money, which gave her security and gave him carte blanche on how he treated us and others. It was stupid on so many levels. To avoid the beatings I started running over and over to any safe place nearby.

My stepfather was a very scary person and he made you always live in fear. None of my friends would come over, he scared us all. Nothing was ever good enough -- he was a control freak supreme and so much more. I tried sports, biking and whatever activities to try to avoid and forget about him. At that time music became my favorite balm and a true place of escape for me. We were in a higher financial class now and we kept to ourselves a lot more. Herb still had hatred for God. He hated his race, the government, anything that seemed to oppress him. He instilled in each of us these beliefs as warnings to us, but it was really his self-hatred and abuse being passed on to a child. Running away became more frequent and so were the beatings amid the sexual abuse. The running was something I did for the next thirty years. It was an insane asylum disguised as an American success story. My father molested me, my sister and anyone he could. If we said anything we were threatened with further harm. Everything was against us.

We would lose friends due to him. We appeared to look like the Huxtables, the family on the Bill Cosby Show on TV, but we were far from it. Having money hid a lot of problems. We had a lack of family identity, pure affection and kindness. It was like we were soldiers in his poisonous army. Increasingly we never saw any extended family and never really knew our heritage. We were more isolated and kept in a prison of his making. He did not allow us to talk about Jesus or our family. He tried to control everything about us. We had economic advantages, but who cared? We were some kind of perverse family unit so the money didn't matter at all. We were people out of hope, social outcasts and dealing with this unexpected place of grief, shame and madness on a daily basis. It felt like slavery or worse to me every day. Mom put us all at risk, maybe her comfort was more important to her than doing what was right. I think it was pride. I think she was trying to show her family that she was right, so to break away from Herb or get a divorce would be her admitting that she was wrong. Was it all so she could prove a point? I still care about my mom deeply, but I have very little respect for how it all went down. Her choices then put us in a no win situation and did a lot of damage.

It did produce one thing. It helped me begin to grow compassion for others. Due to what we went through, we learned to have empathy for what people have to endure in this life. Ironically, it doesn't always work that way, because as people we typically focus on our circumstances, stay connected to the trauma, allow it mess us up and not learn or gain from it. Then we try to medicate it with drugs, alcohol, sex, money, fame, business, religion or whatever else. We understand that life sucks sometimes, but we also see that it's hard to get the treasure from it any other way. You've got to suffer sometimes to get it. The treasure of compassion is always learned the hard way, it's a very good lesson, but not an easy one to learn. It gives you patience and understanding for others that is phenomenal. The cost of it can mess you up if you're not careful. That's what it did for both of us. When you're young and the abuse is piling up around you, it's hard to see the long term value or gauge any benefit from it. Over time your perspective can change and you can appreciate the gift that was given along with the horror, shame or pain that was with it. Usually both exist in any situation as weird as that sounds.

One of the great paradoxes of life is that joy and sorrow can both be present at the same time, in the same situation. You just have to find it. There was an unbelievable firework show in 1976 along the Hudson River on the 4th of July. I felt like it was all for me. What a beautiful scene. It's one of the few things I loved about New York. That and the sports scene. The full time news reporting of so many teams and chances to go in person to see the best teams and players made me run to sports in a new way. It would become another place of refuge for many years. It helped that I was good at it, but I also loved it. The physical exertion helped me process things better and cope with the worthlessness I felt every day. As an abuse survivor, I can't tell you the one thing that saved me, except for this: God had a plan for me and He was committed to me fulfilling it no matter what. Even though I didn't know who He was.

Chapter 7 - Go West Young Man
Rick

After we had moved away, I got an invite to go see my dad when I was 13. His wife Kay was really kind to me. She didn't have to be, but she was. It was weird after six years and cool to be back at the house and my orchard. He was okay, still drinking and smoking too much, but he was decent toward me. I had my old neighborhood back minus the witch. My best friend, Anthony, and his sister, Jane, whom I loved dearly, were next door. I always thought I would marry her, she was cute and sweet, a perfect combination. I spent a lot of that week over at their house jumping off the roof into the pool, playing with the electric trains, playing pool at dad's house, sitting by the waterfall and hanging out.

One day I grabbed Jane's underwear and pulled it up in the back to give her a wedgie. She squealed with delight and we did this several times over the next few days. I would say "George" and yank them up and we laughed and laughed like young lovers can do. Our ribs even got sore from the tickle fights we had. Her panties got a workout and it was the closest thing to sex we could have so we went for it. Unfortunately I had to go back home and that didn't sit too well with me. I saw a life that I could have and wondered why I couldn't have it. It was perfect, everything restored in a moment or so it seemed. The more questions I asked about why, the angrier I got. There was something missing for me. I felt like California was stolen from me and now I had to leave again. My life appeared to be right there before me only to be snatched away again. That pattern would appear over and over for me.

So when I was fourteen I spent much of the summer working out and being a loner. I had friends, but I was on a mission. I wanted to get big and strong. I worked on my hitting every day, lifting weights and footwork for football. I ate peanut butter and honey sandwiches to give me protein and power. This was before supplements and GNC. I worked out hard for at least two hours a day. I was captain of the football team and when baseball season came I was a monster. I was buff and I was focused.

I remember a beautiful girl, Traci, probably the prettiest girl in our junior high. For some reason she was at my baseball game one day. I saw her and I swung as hard as I could, I wanted to hit a home run in her heart! She smiled at me after a big miss. I just smiled and shook my head. It was so funny. One of the kid's parents said, "Just relax and swing easy." So I did. I took a deep breath, looked at Traci, she looked at me and I stepped in the batter's box. I felt like I was swinging a straw and the smooth swing, calm spirit and athletic power all connected and I hit a homer to right center on the next pitch. It was a beautiful shot. I remember crossing home plate and tipping my helmet to Traci. She smiled and she lit up the entire city in that moment. She did something in my heart, too. I wanted her from that day on.

I ended up dominating games throughout the season. I had multiple home run games, I played flawless defense. My batting average was well over .600 that season. I led the league in Home Runs and RBIs, too. I had arrived, we were undefeated and dominating our league. I was on my way to greatness, just like I always believed. Near the end of the season we were playing a Commerce City team and I hit a homer first at bat. Second at bat I hit a double and as I slid into second there was a metal bar above the ground to tie the base onto. It was the first time I had seen one. As I slid into the bag my ankle caught the bar and twisted really weirdly. It hurt instantly. I played on it for a while. My third at bat, I crushed the ball almost out of the entire park which had no fences. I managed to stagger to second base. It would have been a home run twice, but my leg was throbbing. We beat them 21-4 and finished early, but when I got home it killed, so I iced it. No one was home when I got there. My parents never came to one of my games so I sat and waited and waited. Actually Mom did come once when my grandparents were in town. Not too impressive for fourteen years' worth of games. After a few hours of icing Mom and Jerry came home from the bar and she looked at me and got this disgusting look, like what did you do now?

I hated her so much. She had to take me to the hospital and I ended up in a cast for six weeks. All Stars were starting the next week. I got ripped off again. I ended up fracturing my ankle in six places. Tiny little cracks in the bone, but damaging none the less. I went to the first practice with the All Starts on crutches. Our team was undefeated and we looked like we were unstoppable, too, since 80% of the All Stars were my team. I couldn't go back after that, there was a huge hole in the team, our dream and my heart. It was a sucky end to such a promising new season. I worked hard and now it was all for nothing, again.

High school was coming, maybe I had that to look forward to. Get healed up, be the captain of the football team, there were still dreams to pursue. My mom had another surprise in store for me though. This one would change my path forever. She got a new job at a bank in Arvada and we moved again. This time going away from Traci and all the guys I knew. There was a great path that was before me. I knew everybody and was in it to win it, ready to take my place and dominate. Now I had to start all over, again. We moved a lot and I knew the drill, but it still sucked ass.

So I went to Arvada West High School, it was a step up from Northglenn and Thornton where I had spent the last six years. I met the head football coach, he was my counselor, and life looked good for me and then I was assigned to start school in October because they were on a year round schedule. What? I was pissed. I waited for a call for football practice, it never came. Once again, disappointment had arrived. What was I going to do for two months? There was a little bar called the Eastlake Inn that my mom liked. What a dump! I started bartending there a few times when I was fifteen. My body was healed, but not the rest of me. I was having trouble understanding why everything seemed to be against me all the time. Could it go well just once? I was going to yet another new school and I was the new kid for the tenth time. Sometimes that was an advantage. People would think, hey you're new, exciting or interesting and fasten themselves on to you. That's especially true if you're a hunky guy, which I was. Big and strong, maybe, but still not confident at all. So it was another exercise in trying to find my niche, my place, my whatever. It was easy to have doubts when things were going sideways all the time. I went into gym class and deadlifted about 500 pounds the first day. That certainly got the attention of everyone. Not bad for a Sophomore.

I had some notoriety, but it wasn't enough to overcome my feelings of inadequacy. I never felt good enough, it was always something I had to deal with, even before I could give it a name. Because of what had happened over the years, I was struggling to believe that anything good would happen. It played out over and over in my life. I didn't know what to do so I gave up playing football, which I loved and was really good at, because I didn't have any way to get in. I hate what was taken from me, but I've spent many years trying to combat failure and making the old mindsets go away. It's so hard when you can't break free, even if you want to. What is the key to doing that? You have to change the way you think. I took me a long time to learn it. You have to hold on to hope and believe for the good even when the circumstances say different. Even when life sucks. Our brains make pathways of connection that begin in infancy. We learn to process life a certain way and once those pathways are established we have a quick road to travel on for thoughts and decisions. That doesn't always mean they are healthy paths or the right roads. Sometimes all they are is the fastest way for our brains to process stress, decisions, choices and all kinds of things. Taking the time to retrain your mind into a new way of thinking can be stressful, even difficult, but it will yield amazing changes in your life and it really is a key in setting you free and keeping you in that freedom for a long time.

So because of what I believed I was stuck not playing the game I loved. For years, I had to overcome my expectation that everything in my life was always going to be a struggle and I couldn't do that, not yet. Difficult is okay, but if that's all you ever see, it can steal your joy or your hope if you're not aware. You have to learn the mental toughness required to overcome the onslaught of life against you. Staying in my expectation of doom was really dumb, but sometimes it was easier for me to go back to what I knew even if it hurt me. If there's nobody to help, mentor you or support you, it's difficult at best. Nobody wants that kind of life. Still sometimes it finds you or catches you unaware. You really have to be intentional in what you think about yourself, what you do and what you say or you'll probably never get over the garbage. Find a light and shine it on yourself and maybe you can find healing all the way to a cellular level. You have to understand how amazing you are, how special. No matter what has happened to you, you are wonderful and purposeful, you are beautiful just the way you are. If someone said horrible things about you or you believe them about yourself, please do both of us a favor and stop letting those things define you. You are a unique person, you have value and there are things only you can do in this world. We need you! You are perfectly made, despite the flaws. It's the truth! The words you speak are key. If you confess that you're stupid, no good, ugly or whatever then that's what you will be. It's really taking your words and your thoughts about yourself under your own control and making them into what you want them to be. We often react to situations as a way to deal with our lives, but I'm suggesting we be proactive about defining our own lives, not letting situations, failures or circumstances do that for us. Others may have said things about you that linger or make it hard, but it's up to you to grab that thing by the throat and deal with it. Only you can do it! I believe you can actually change your history, change your destiny, your DNA and become something different but it's not likely to be an easy process or a quick one.

Mom was still living her different kind of life, but once she left Jerry she actually began to heal some. Her mindset went from survival mode to one of thinking, breathing and dreaming. She was a smart lady, pretty and had a lot of good work traits, too. It's hard for those to come out when you're trying to stay alive. She started a new job at Colorado National Bank and finally found her groove. Within a year she was lead teller, within two years she was Vice President of Operations, a bank officer and making twice as much money as she ever made in her life. She was a ridiculously good saver, so we still lived a pretty spartan lifestyle, but I started seeing her smile somedays and though she still spent most evenings at the bar, she wouldn't drink much, just enjoying the atmosphere around her, socializing and dancing. There was a bar called the Urban Cowgirl close to the bank. It was a mom and pop family place and filled with genuine people who really cared about each other. Very unique in that bar setting, which was more likely a place to share misery and regrets with a host of lost and lonely losers. In some ways, it was a place of refuge and support for her. She wasn't angry all the time.

53

It was refreshing to see her smile. The trauma of her domestic violence was easing a bit. Time is a good healer in that way. She found life apart from the foulness of Jerry. So did I.

I was a good athlete and made the basketball and baseball teams during that Sophomore year. I was really good. I even got a part time job at Dairy Queen where several of the cutest high school girls worked, too. Heaven on earth, cuties and ice cream! The turbulent years of Jerry and losing my dad, were starting to fade a bit and I could breathe again in some ways. I still had a lot to process and found myself somewhat outgoing, almost happy-go-lucky, even to the cute cheerleaders at the new high school. I was ready to get serious about my dreams again, then fate found a new way to crap on me. My grandfather, the only male figure in my life got diagnosed with colon cancer. He had smoked for forty years, but quit when he saw a film about how your lungs get damaged from smoking at the county fair. True story! We went and saw him that summer and he was fine. He even bought Grandma a new house that she loved and fixed it up nice for her. I loved Grandpa, he was eclectic like me. He painted signs, did carpentry, played in a band, did repair work, really an all-around handyman who could do virtually anything to pay some bills. He had a big smile and a little bit of mischievous in him. Some of it was cool, but some of it was not. I always wondered if he fooled around on Grandma or molested little kids, something wasn't quite right in there, but naively, I admired him anyway. His diagnosis went from bad to worse. Those years wreaked havoc on him and soon he was in Mexico as a last ditch effort to find a cure. He died within six months of diagnosis.

There had seemed to be a slight break in the clouds in my life, but new clouds were gathering on the horizon where I could not see them. It was then that I discovered that I had friends at school who smoked marijuana and it was easy to hang out at each other's houses and smoke it whenever we wanted to. My grandfather's death left me angry. I had stopped pot so I could train, but I had lost my zeal a bit and we started smoking it when we could after school. We all worked part time jobs so we could pay for it. We didn't have to smoke it every day, but pretty soon we were. It was really stupid in a lot of ways, but a lot of people were doing it and it did make laughter much easier. At this point I needed some laughter. I felt like a part of me was taken, he was the first person close to me who died. I missed him, even though we weren't super close. My friends, we all shared similar stories of loss and shame, so we all gravitated to each other. Misery loves company right?

I wonder how many of them are still smoking pot to this day. I know of a few who are and I think really dude? When are you going to grow up and put that shit down? It's been over thirty years, come on! I call that the marshmallow response. It's where you have problems, issues or challenges to overcome and you simply self-medicate instead. I can understand doing it for a little while, but not for thirty or forty years. That shows a special level of cowardice in some ways and a sadly disconnected life in other ways. I guess I take it personally because I've seen my brothers and my cousins do exactly that. Potentially great lives wasted in a haze of drugs, alcohol and unforgiveness. I think most of us have something to forgive from our past. It may be a harsh word, a horrible violation or another level of neglect or abuse. The point is, if we don't get over it, who will? No one will do the hard work for us and make life better by waving a magic wand. It doesn't work like that. We have to own our stuff, even the trash pile and then we can do something about it. If you ignore it, it doesn't go away. In fact, it usually gets bigger. My brother George was that way. He lived a vagabond life with no forgiveness. He was an amazing guitarist for years. Played with a bunch of famous rock star guys before he got whacked out on drugs. He died while I was writing this book and it felt like a big loss. He got cancer really bad and lasted about eight months. Some of this book was written while sitting on his couch while he slept. I miss him. He wasn't quite Stevie Ray Vaughn good, but he was close. He played many styles from Baroque to Rock, from Jazz to Flamenco. He was quite a guy. I just finished cleaning out his apartment. It made me think. What is life for? To enjoy, be amazed and take it all in. He didn't do that. Another life lost to unforgiveness. He had so much potential, but the years of drugs got to him. He had a skill, a talent and now the world will never know it. I miss you brother, rest in peace.

In high school, we thought pot was cool, we just had to be sure to be smart about who we bought it from. Our regular dealer was searched by the cops and somehow they didn't find the stash he was sitting on under the couch cushions, so we were done with him. The next guy we used was a lunatic supreme. Scott was an ex-military guy who loved weapons and worked at KFC with a friend of mine Jeff. He had a whole armory in his apartment so we never would do anything to piss him off. He was close to going thermonuclear most of the time anyway. One night he asked us to come with him because he wanted to break into the National Guard Armory and steal weapons from there. He promised us each one weapon out of the cache he was after. We told him, let us think about it and left. We never ever went back to see him again. I ended up spending my junior year in a funk. Our JV basketball coach changed and the job was given to the Varsity soccer coach whose version of basketball was to make us run all practice long. It sucked and most of us didn't last a month. Then my grandfather was getting really bad, so quitting was easy. No one came to see why I wasn't playing baseball either, did they not care? I became friends with Adam, he was a left handed pitcher and really good. I should have played, I would have lettered and we would have been really good. Adam and I smoked pot together, a lot of the athletes did. Those who didn't drank and chewed tobacco. It was everywhere, I guess that made it easy. We were all nursing away some pain or just bored and trying to make our own dangerous fun. Life was good or so we thought. I came back and lettered during senior year in baseball, but the coaches were weird when you didn't play the year before or in the summer.

After high school, we were close to the heat, but we were stupid. It was easy for us to see the wisdom in dealing drugs to pay for our habit. Buying drugs was expensive, if you sold them yourself, you were earning money to pay for them and wasn't that brilliant? No, not really. When you're eighteen the rules change and pretty soon everyone's got a target on their back. Getting charged as an adult is way different. So now we were operating and making deals as we needed to. It was fun to be the king, or at least think we were. I remember paying rent in pot at one apartment complex we lived in. Money talks! All that changed one day, when the newest dealer we used got busted. He had several pounds of pot and he ended up doing many years of hard time in prison. Intent to distribute is no joke and it scared the shit out of us. One of my brother in laws friends got busted with a few pounds and he blew his brains out rather than go to prison! That was a tough month. We shut down the network and took a deep breath. We had been at his place just a few hours before it all went down. It was a felony charge and 15 years of hard time in prison is pretty normal as far as that charge goes. We got lucky.

Chapter 8 - White Privilege
Marcus

We spent a few years in New York and it was a crazy place! When we moved away I was glad on some level. Herb had tried to hit on almost every female in the states of Missouri and New York. The Big Apple was a haven for disco. It was Billy Dee Williams, Kool menthol cigarettes, Colt 45 beer and Studio 54. I didn't miss the Catholic school with the yellow turtleneck uniforms, the mean kids and the nuns. I was learning that not all whites were bad, no matter how full of hatred Herb tried to fill my head. That was New York! Hello Virginia! Home to eight Presidents, the largest shipyards in the world and my next phase of life. I had no idea how a military lifestyle looked, worked or that it even existed. Virginia was like that, but in New York there was such a diverse population, that people tended to get along. It wasn't as segregated or racist as other places like Virginia Beach. Herb did management training classes and got a promotion to open a new branch and be the manager at GMAC overseeing about 200 employees. We had a new house built from the ground up. We were living large, right? It was 1980 and we were barely moved in when the Rams and the Steelers played in the Super Bowl. My sister Yasmine was born the day Ronald Reagan got shot in March of 1981.

Herb was working hard and the stress made him even harsher than ever. His true heart was coming out. He had never addressed the past and he was unable to get any joy out of life, even chasing women and having all this money wasn't enough for him. So work became everything to him, even at Christmas time, he would be upstairs not really spending time with us. Just making that money and letting the past define him.

Virginia Beach is where I really started to learn about the different classes of people: economically, racially and culturally. There were poor people and rich people of all different races. There were many Vietnamese, Filipino, and Asians in our area, which was a totally new culture to me. The military and naval settings were unique, too. You had many families with a dad gone for six months at a time serving aboard a ship or overseas. So most of the families were single mom types, but not really. No dads around meant more cheating and trying to fill the loneliness of those extended trips, it was another strange version of life. It was a kind of caste system of the haves and have nots. Race played a big factor, but so did economics.

They built a new GMAC building near Mount Trashmore and Herb was even more dysfunctional, spending all his time working and freaking out. The longer hours meant we would eat dinner later at like 8:00 p.m.. We should have been in bed by then but Mom made us wait for him. When things got stupid and I was in fear, there was this abandoned building I found for a while. It was a place of escape where I could be indoors and away from Herb. I would even hang out in apartment building lobbies and sleep on the floor. At the age of ten, how did no one notice a kid sleeping in the lobby? I felt like a war-torn refuge. I would walk the canal late at night, sleep outside and then still go to school with the same clothes on, just to avoid my dad.

One thing I had learned by now was that you can't let anyone know what you're going through. They could also use it against you or think less of you. So how do you deal with a broken heart? Good question. It was becoming more and more survival mode for me. It was fight or flight. Do whatever it takes to get by and not let anybody else in. The wall you build to protect yourself becomes the prison wall that keeps you in. It's a place of darkness and you think it makes you safe, but it makes you a prisoner and an isolated one. You start to become two different people. The one you are when you have to be and the one you are when there's no one around. I was becoming my step father without even realizing it. What a mess! He was not a parent, he was barely even present by now. Yet his tyranny and his fury were ever-present for me. I was convinced that when you shared something emotional like this abuse to others, you got stomped on, so no one could ever know. It was a vicious circle and it led to the first of many times where self-sabotage would come in to play. I couldn't be a genius, or do great at school or people would notice me. It's a curse to play the fool but somehow you convince yourself it's the right way to go! In reality, being myself could have helped me so much. People would have noticed, maybe even cared for me and helped me through. I was cutting off valuable people in my life by not being able to share the real me. Some people may have hurt me when I showed my vulnerability, but some would have been wonderful, too! It's hard to be emotionally unprotected, but it could have saved me a lot of trouble. I was trying to protect myself, but it wasn't working. I was just getting deeper and deeper into the quicksand and it was sucking me down quickly. In Virginia Beach we had a new house, with better cars and more money. Economic privileges mean nothing if you don't have a place of safety or love. White kids made fun of my blond, curly hair and always wanted to touch it like I was a circus freak or something. They liked me because I was one of them in their eyes. Black kids mocked the way I talked like a white person and they called me a white boy or Redbone. Some of the kids called me "Nigonky", half Nigger, half Honky! They said I was a half breed so I had to fight a lot out of anger and frustration over who I was. I didn't know and they didn't know who I really was. This would get me in trouble at school acting out and I would suffer another beating at home. So I would do more mischief, runaway, then get caught by Herb and then beat again. I didn't know any different way to live. The vicious circle of sadness was exhausting to say the least!

There were a lot of Navy families in the area and a lot from the Midwest. They only knew the word nigger to describe us, so this brought on more challenges and fights. I hated that word and I still do. It meant that you were less than human. Somewhere between piss ant and dog. That was not me, but I had no reservoir to draw from and I was starting to drown. My stomach would hurt. I was nervous all the time. I hated Herb and we were clashing every chance we got. We were like two wrestlers in the ring, unable to let each other go. Unwilling to separate for a moment to breathe.

Remember that Virginia used to be the head of the Confederacy. Richmond was the Confederate capital and it's a very racist place even to this day. Arthur Ashe in his autobiography talks about growing up in Richmond. He was the #1 Men's Tennis player in the world in 1968 and the only black man to win the singles title at Wimbledon. He won by defeating defending champion Jimmy Connors. He was known for his great sportsmanship and calm demeanor. He was also the first black to win the US Open, Australian Open and National Junior Indoor singles tennis titles. Governor Douglas Wilder of Virginia had become a friend over the years to Arthur and when he died in 1993 at the age of 49, Wilder allowed his coffin to lie in estate at the governor's mansion. Governor Wilder was the first black mayor of Richmond and first black Governor of Virginia. He was the first black Governor of any U.S. state when he was elected in 1990. He won the Bronze Star Medal during the Korean War and graduated from Virginia Union University and Howard University law school. These are our examples to follow. Work hard, get an education, sacrifice, do well and gain opportunities to help yourself and your fellow man. If our cause is just, we will win every time. Every single time! God knows it won't be easy. Why do we even think that? Nothing is easy in this life especially trying to succeed under this weight. Our black culture needs a wake-up call to moral purity and a good work ethic.

Nothing can derail a life like poor moral behavior, just ask Shawn Kemp about that. He was a six-time NBA All-Star and by the age of 28, he had fathered seven children with six different women. He was arrested in 2005 for drug possession and plead guilty. He was the youngest player in the NBA when he was drafted at 19 years old. The Sonics had a great team and Xavier McDaniel became his mentor and friend as well as Gary Payton, Ricky Pierce, Nate McMillan and Eddie Johnson. They won 64 games in 1995-96 season and lost in six games to the Michael Jordan led Bulls in the NBA Finals. Shawn had weight problems and even entered drug rehab at one point. An absentee father, but later he reconnected with his son Shawn Kemp, Jr. before his junior year in high school and he has made an effort to be there for him in basketball and in life. His son went to the University of Washington. Kemp Sr. made a lot of mistakes along the way, but he reconnected with his son at a critical point. We don't have to do it perfect, but we need to try and do what's right. Hats off to Shawn for being there! He made a change and changed the direction for his son. I wish a few more fathers would do that! There were many times I needed this kind of help in my life. For a long time it never came. Hopelessness came in its place. That is a horrible companion to have.

Finally after many days of running away and petty crimes like stealing bikes, destroying mailboxes by fire, and such, Herb finally had enough. So I was sent to a military boarding school in Fork Union, VA. Right there on James Madison Highway. I didn't want to go. It was a totally new experience. Everyone had money. A lot more than we did. So much structure, it was a culture shock to me! Being smart was never the problem, it was being abandoned and having to fight the racism that abounded in this all white, blue blood school. Deep in the heart of redneck country as my stepdad would say. Our showers were in the barracks and there was a hierarchy based on who was most developed as a man, not just in sports, studies and money. It was a complex new world. At first I felt the punishment of being sent away. I was eleven years old, immature, processing my PTSD, one of the few black students in an all-white school and I was alone. Really alone for the first time. Some of the guys were racist and not too excited to see me, some were indifferent and most just thought, yeah whatever dude, get used to it, we all had to. I found that being away from my sisters, my mom, and I what I knew, created a lot of anxiety in me. I wasn't able to protect them from Herb and my wandering mind lead to all kinds of thoughts, fears and sorrow. Some days I wanted to jump out the window. There was no way to do anything about it. Believe me, I was glad to get away from Herb, but I missed all my friends. It's where I really fell in love with sports, history and music. I needed something to hang on to.

We wore these gray uniforms with shiny brass buckles. I would wake up in the morning, in your mind you're a little kid remember, you would shower with the other boys. That was new. We had a shower that was in the middle of the dorm and you had your own room that was in a wing. You had to have the gray floor tiles clean, ready to eat off of. You did that in the morning by 6 o'clock and you got dressed up in your uniform of the day. You had to have your bunk and personal items in shipshape and Bristol fashion. A certain perfection was expected and also your clothes had to be clean and have straight lines. Everything had to be done a certain way, not just any way. There was discipline, self-control, character building, precision and more. All valuable things, but some days it was worse than Herb, but with none of the toxic side effects. Then they would call for us breakfast and we marched to the mess hall to eat. It was hard at first, but over time I came to appreciate the preciseness of it. I started to get used to it after a while. I felt like a white kid in many ways, because I knew that world, but I didn't know how to be black in a white world. Especially one raised by a monster.

This place had the best of the best attending there. For a small fee of $40,000 a year I was hanging out with future Ivy leaguers headed to Yale, Dartmouth and Harvard, future professional athletes like Vinny Testaverde and Chris Washburn, natural businessmen and politicians in training. It took a long time to see it for what it really was. This was a chance to see my potential, to thrive and prosper, not just survive. I did well at school. I excelled in swimming, too, but my poor behavior led to demerits and loss of privileges. When that happened I had to dress in fatigues, combat boots, a rain coat and start marching. I marched forever some days. I was always getting in fights. This is where I learned about white privilege for the first time. They had money, land, cool toys, trust funds, horses, yachts and the understanding that they were different. They thought they were better than you and most of them let you know that they believed it. Some were just really great guys. I had a roommate from Boston who turned me on to the music coming out of there like Boston, Journey, the Cars, the Clash, Aerosmith and so much more. It was very therapeutic.

When you're rich you don't worry. When you're poor you problem solve. I wasn't sure who I was. I was indeed black privilege, a very small minority, but I felt poor and wretched on the inside and in this crowd. The loneliness and homesick feelings were getting difficult, but so was the thought of going back home. Consciously, I tried to get in trouble there so I would not have to go home during school breaks. I loved the freedom of not having to see my father, more than the challenge of missing my Mom and sisters. I saw a different kind of life when I sometimes went with my friends from Fork Union to their places on day passes. Some of these families had big estates with rolling hills, stables with horses and houses out of Better Mansions and Gardens! I watched them interact with each other, I saw how loving and gentle some of the parents were. At first, it made me sad for my lack of love, but after a while, I realized that there was something different out there. I always hoped there was, but it was really tough to visualize without seeing it demonstrated before me. Once it was, I had renewed hope for a better life. That's the best advice there is, show your kids that there is something better out there. You can grow up in the projects, but you don't have to stay there. There are places to see, people to meet, so much to do in life. Travel, read books, experience different cultures. It makes you a more balanced and well-rounded person, even dreamers of dreams like we are.

I loved learning and this was the cream of the crop for classmates, teachers and counselors. I was befriended by a few of the staff, they recognized something was missing for me. I think at first, they thought it was just me being black or young or lonely, but they really paid attention like no one had before and it excited me. Somebody cared, that was a nice new twist. I used to listen to Casey Kasem on Sundays. I loved the Top Ten and I followed the radio show like it was my lighthouse. I would come back home and everybody would talk about all the fun they had in public school. Herb must have really wanted to get rid of me if he was willing to pay that much. My mind was messed up thinking it through. The randomness of the thoughts were arduous. I had so much emotion inside me. Later on I learned about the fight or flight mechanism. I was in it all the time. Just trying to find some way to survive it all, by whatever means necessary. I had never been to church before Fork Union and one day they asked me to pray for the meal and I said, "Rub-a-dub-dub, thanks for the grub, yeah God!" The Captain beat me down for my lack of respect to his God that he loved. I spent a lot of time marching extra duty for that one. After this event, another time of sabotaging my trip home for break, my counselor called my dad and asked him to come up to talk. Success had covered the bad behavior for a long time for both of us. It still does that in the black community, we can do whatever we want as long as the money rolls in or whatever, but this time the cat was out of the bag.

Those two years were challenging and great in some ways, but when I was twelve I got kicked out and I had to go back with my family. The beatings and running away continued but I would still go to school. I had a desire to learn and I knew there was a future for me there in education, but it was getting harder and harder. Fork Union helped me see that education could change your path. We even won the city football championship in 7th grade. The double life was getting more difficult to navigate. The anger, harder to control. The emotions tougher to manage especially when I found out I had a biological father. As far as I knew it was Herb, but my birth certificate said different. He wasn't my real father after all. It was Anthony Hill. Another piece to the puzzle. Imagine my reaction, pure rage! When I would fight, I was a maniac. I would bite people, whatever to beat them and punish them. I was very scary. Anger, heartbreak, disappointment and loneliness were in control and I was not.

Chapter 9 - Back to St. Louis
Marcus

The summer when I was thirteen I went back to St. Louis to meet my birthfather. By now, life was crazy all the time. Herb started being gone longer days as his job demanded more time and his double life began to develop. He was starting a second family on the side. He was around less which was nice. He had another lady he lived with part of the time and then he lived with us, too. She was the ultimate prize to him, a white woman! Eventually he even had a child with her. I found all this out much later of course. I was glad to get away from this insane asylum for the summer. I needed the break. St. Louis is where I learned a whole new way of life. I suddenly saw white privilege from a whole new perspective, as though it was me! When I got to St. Louis, the majority of my relatives lived in the projects. They were not town homes like I thought. This was the wrong place at the wrong time activity center. I was hip in my nice clothes and cool shoes, but nobody else was like me. There I had cousins dealing drugs and waving guns. My Aunt and her husband were struggling due to infidelity. There were deceptive characters all around. It was a new bitter ocean to navigate. There were no role models, no marriages valued, few fathers and no examples to follow. I had to learn discernment the hard way. One cousin had no dad and did drugs with his mom. Other cousins never married, living a life of shame and affliction as ghetto superstars and low level thugs. It was a sharp contrast to me, this inner city minefield. It was intriguing and surreal at that same time.

They introduced me to this weird concept called layaway. My family used credit cards to buy whatever we wanted. In the projects, they didn't have those luxuries, but they could set something aside and make payments on it until they could buy it. What? Dealing drugs and cheating was the norm, how do you overcome that? My cousins challenged me to see if I was "black enough" to sell drugs, do drugs or fight. I suddenly did not like St. Louis too much anymore, the weird vibe there was getting personal. With the inner city pools full of gross lab experiments, I started looking for other things to do there. I really liked riding my bike to the Arch. In St. Louis, I started to see the world differently. I encountered generational poverty for the first time. Not just a little bit, but abject poverty. I saw living in public housing, the projects, the lack of privilege, no initiative, no wisdom to get better, no understanding of how to change your circumstances, no motivation and how it had played out for many generations! I had seen the good life, the privilege of my Fork Union friends. Here there was no privilege, no possibilities, no hope. It really opened my eyes to a new side of life and the huge needs that were out there. Hope is a powerful thing and it's missing a lot in America. I had a new calling.

Later that year, Michael Jackson's Thriller album came out and took the world by storm. I have a family connection to it all. My cousin Ola Ray was the girl who played Michael Jackson's girlfriend in the Thriller video. She was in a few movies, too, including Beverly Hills Cop II, 48 Hours, 10 To Midnight, Fear City and Night Shift! She became famous after being the Playboy Playmate of the Month in June of 1980, at the age of 19. In 1992 she was arrested for possession of cocaine. Ups and downs, just like the rest of our family. We all have seen some struggles but you learn to love people no matter what they do. I am proud of my cousin and I love her. I'm glad she made a name for herself. She was at-risk, just like me and found a way out.

I moved around St. Louis quite a bit that summer and made myself some money by selling bomb pops for cash. I got to see family, but it was a culture shock in so many ways. I hadn't seen them in years and I wasn't used to everybody being black! That might sound weird. So many times there were just a few of us, but here, we were all over the place. Everybody was black! I started seeing the world differently again. There was a lot of acting out with the blacks I met. People again said I acted white, so I learned to fit in better, but then I wondered why. Another double life was brewing. I would fight with my cousins and we would get aggressive and we would strike back against each other and anyone else we thought was disrespecting us. This was the poor inner city and dads are usually looked at like some kind of enemy or scourge. Mothers try to run the show as best they can. The fathers are absent, usually playing around, in jail or looking for the next score. It's no wonder we're falling behind! We got to return to the right way of doing life as families again. I struggle with being a father even to this day. All the absentee fathers know what I mean. Somehow you want to be there, maybe not all the time, but you feel it. Then you're awkward or not welcome, pretty soon it's too weird, too emotional or just too hard to deal with. They want child support but then you can't see the kids, or they use them against you. I feel you fellas, I know how it goes down. They want to rule it all and you get whatever scraps they throw you. How is that working out by the way? At least there are some rules in place now, it used to be if the father was gone, he's gone. Now the kids can have some chance to know their dad. Living in a single mom family is the hardest thing ever. You feel unsafe, unloved, underappreciated at times. It's a tough life, economically and socially. You were looked down on and treated poorly. If you were the kid with old shoes or jeans patches on your knees the other kids would let you know it.

There were lines within the city that when you crossed them, you felt the change. The atmosphere was actually different. It was where the whiter sections were. It wasn't always a better feeling, but sometimes it was. It was tangible, you could sense it, almost see it or touch it or taste it. It's hard to explain. On my bike I was exploring and figuring out how to travel safely and smartly through town. I also learned that nice cars mattered. In the projects, everybody was poor, but the guy dealing drugs he had some nice wheels and a wad of cash in his pocket. He was the man! Who doesn't want to be the man? I spent the whole summer there. I learned a lot watching the cheaters, the thugs and drug dealers and going to the pawn shop. This was a new experience, too. So many people had just a few things of value and were taken advantage of, either by paying high fees on the pawn shop loans or by losing our stuff for pennies on the dollar when we couldn't pay the ransom. There needs to be a new way to do this business without stealing people's thing or charging them 100% interest. How about a pawn shop for the people? Make it into a helpful thing not a license to steal from the poor. So many ideas. We've got to change some things and I mean soon.

My Aunt Mabel arranged for me to meet my birth dad, he was light skinned like me. He looked like me, I wanted to hang with him and see his world. It was a whole new adventure. Some of the blanks started to be filled in, but a lot more questions started coming up. Part of me was glad of course to see him and part of me was mad. So much of my life was defined by Herb and now to meet my real dad, my sperm donor, was opening a whole new can of worms in so many ways. All the feelings were starting to come up and it was going to be a day of reckoning. I went out to a family plot of land near Kinloch, Missouri. My great, great Grandma Simmons had eight kids in a one bedroom house there. The Simmons family had a restaurant there called Shaq Pappy's, some real barbecue. Forget Kansas City, it was good enough to make you want to hurt yourself! It was the first black city settled and incorporated in Missouri. It's still there close to Ferguson, northwest of St. Louis. It's close to Cool Valley where we had our first nice house. What an irony, those two worlds so close together. Kinloch is a virtual ghost town now, a pile of rubble except for a few houses. If you like the Mad Max movies, you'll love Kinloch. There's a bit of that post-apocalyptic feel to be sure. At one time there were 10,000 residents, now you might find 300. If you look real hard.

When I got back from St. Louis, I noticed a neighbor girl had moved in. She was cute and white, just about my age and became my friend instantly. The ultimate prize right? Our parents would not allow us to play together but we found a way to hang out still. This was when I saw the effect of white and black culture intertwined. Virginia Beach was a utopia for us youngsters who were figuring it all out together. Just do not tell your folks! I did not tell, and neither did she. In the Virginia Beach suburbs, we were mischievous which fed right into my rebellious spirit. I was always the master mind and the first to throw a punch. Do not let the light skin fool you! I had all this pent up aggression against my Dad that I spewed out on others when confronted. No one was going to hurt me! I had no boundaries. I would steal beer and sell it at parties. I claimed I had a fake ID, then I would pocket the money. It was a way to hang out with the cool crowd and try to navigate the emotions of my new found worlds. St. Louis had opened my eyes in so many ways. There were lies and secrets, there were racists, despots and thugs. Of course, there was still Herb here, too. I was slowly learning how dysfunctional my Mom's family really was. It was very female dominated. Mom had some wisdom and some brains, but because of her background, it was hard to sustain. In her family there was substance abuse, heroin, weed and booze at every family party. That's even still true to this day. The man can do whatever he wants and get away with it. Self-medicating, selfish attitudes, having eight kids and not being married. Is this how all of black culture is? It sure was in my version of it. Having a family and doing what's right is near the bottom of the list.

Trying to become a man in the midst of guys gone wild during the 70s and 80s was a real battle. There were sexually wild men and women everywhere and it's very hard to become a man of character in a world like that. Harder still in a world where you're left to figure it all out for yourself. The disco era was in full swing and the use of cocaine was rising faster than an Arizona thermometer in July. All the poor behavior of St. Louis was everywhere. By this time, Herb hit on any woman, even in front of Mom. He had money and power, a double life, so in his mind, the rules did not apply to him. He would say things like, "Hey honey, how's your body treating you?" He even wore underwear that said, "The home of the whopper." True story. His mindset was women are beneath you, they are a commodity to be used as needed, not someone to be cherished or even cared about. Little did I know that there was a mighty crusader fighting for me. My great Aunt Geraldine was a prayer warrior and she was fighting for the family to get free and to be safe. I believe her prayers are the only thing that kept us all alive.

Chapter 10 - Happy Birthday
Rick

One day when I was five, my sister Colleen and I were in the front yard and she was talking to a friend of hers and the next thing you know, I was out by the street with my thumb out. She had taught me so well that I knew how to hitchhike like a champ, even when we didn't need a ride. Another time we hopped onto two different motorcycles at the tiny mall we had and they rode us home. It was my first and last time of accidentally touching the exhaust pipes with my leg. That burn lasted for a while. Mom was so loaded I don't think she ever noticed it. Risky behavior is easy when no one notices or cares. Another time my sister had friends over and they were all smoking pot and I was there since she was my caretaker. Apparently one of the guys who was over thought it would be cool to teach me how to smoke a joint. So here I am a little kid smoking pot like a champ, what kind of messed up family does this? My sister would defend me from Mom but not from her friends. What a messed up kid she was, too. I still love her though, without her there is very little chance I survive my childhood.

The hardest part is, now marijuana is legal in Colorado and a few other states. They say only adults but I see people smoking it at the park all the time, even kids. It is a stupid mess. Last time I checked, Federal Law supersedes State Law, so even if it's voted in, the Federal Law prohibiting it should be the law. The President and the Attorney General will not enforce the law, which is the main function of their branch of government. How have they not been impeached already or at least called to task on this? It's the main function of the executive branch to enforce the law, yet they refuse. Maybe we should impeach them ourselves. We all need to change course, this country is a mess because everyone is doing what is right in their own eyes. That's what killed off the Roman Empire and every other super power of the past. When the people get so strong, wealthy and lazy, that they think they can do whatever they want and feel entitled to their folly, it's a short trip to destruction.

When I was sixteen my grandfather got cancer. He was my Mom's dad and the only male in my life who was consistent. I never knew my dad's family at all. So the stress of watching him slowly die a painful death from colon cancer took a lot of my joy at that time. I gave up sports and work and was just miserable. I started smoking cigarettes and pot again to deal with it. Life was weird again, another turn into the exit lane instead of the fast lane. I always admired Grandpa, he was a renaissance man like me. He wasn't perfect, but he was family. Sometimes that's enough. He was German, born in America, but from German immigrants. He had a taste for food that I would call strange. He liked things like blood sausage. It looked like intestines or something. He swore up and down it was delicious! Another treat of his was Limburger cheese. If you have never tried it, I think you should. I'm guessing it tastes like what it smells like. How can I describe it? It's a combination of baby diarrhea and old cheese. I think it's the German version of Kim Chee or something. Anyway, he would open the package and the smell would fill the whole house. We would run outside to avoid it, because once it was in your nose, it wouldn't leave. He always wanted us to try it and even tried to give us money to do it. One day he offered my cousin Tiffany a princely sum of five cents to taste this magnificent creation. After much prodding he got her to try it. She was maybe six years old. She put a little bite on her tongue and her face went into a frown. She kept her mouth open trying to get it out, but it stuck to her tongue. She was gagging and her knees started buckling. She was rocking back and forth and she finally went and spit it out. Her sister Brook and I were rolling on the floor. She started washing her tongue in the sink from the faucet and Grandpa said, "It's good, isn't it? Yer Goot!"

I don't know if I ever laughed that hard before. I still miss him today and I remember each birthday that passes. Next year he would have been 110. Cancer got him when he was 75 and I miss his big smile, it was genuine and infectious. Walking through his death was difficult, but I remember the good things, like climbing on the roof of the garage and picking Apricots right off the tree and eating them or helping him paint signs. He polished me a set of cow horns that I still have to this day. His workshop was a wonderland. Tools, wood, machines, all kinds of unexplored areas. I never got a lot of time with him, but I am thankful for what I had. Isn't that what life is for? It's in the difficult moments that we learn to be humble and grateful for whatever good things we do have. There's plenty of other stuff to focus on, but to what end? I'm learning that gratitude is better than regret.

My mom was such a cheap ass, but she wanted to buy me a car for my 18th birthday. I saw a beautiful Mercury Cougar with the three taillights that lit up separately. It was cherry. Dark blue with white interior, pretty fast and a chick magnet, just what I needed. I was so excited. I had worked hard at Burger King to save up for it. I had long since lost my Traci, but I was trying to make up for it with new friends Kim, Tracy, Nikki and Andra. So even though I had the money, my mom said no. She offered to give me $500 toward a car that she thought was better somehow. So I was going to turn eighteen and a co-worker of hers had a used car for sale. A beautiful 1966 VW bug with a roll top sun roof. What a piece of crap! I felt like the biggest loser on the Biggest Loser. I took it and hated her even more. She was so happy. It was a clutch and it took me a while to learn how to drive one again. Her friend Goldie had taught me when I was fourteen. She said, "You'll always want a clutch car when you get a fast one, so you control the gearing and the acceleration, and it's more fun to go fast." It was beautifully said, and she was absolutely right and a nice lady.

So I was turning a corner in my bug, heading home one day and I took the corner a little fast and as I turned it started sliding. I hit the curb and the VW rolled. The sunroof was open and for a few seconds I wondered if I was going to scrape my skull off on the pavement. The slow motion feeling of going upside down was a really remarkable experience. It was like time had almost stopped for a bit and then went back to full speed again. It was surreal and I guess I'm lucky to be alive. Thankfully I was okay, just a few bruises, but the car was totaled. The axle was bent and the top of the tire was pushed out five inches from where it should be. The guys at the body shop just laughed. I should have scrapped it and moved on but I tried to fix it. It was too expensive so I let them have it. Good riddance! I owned it for about two weeks. Just another mess to clean up. The Cougar had sold, so that was not an option. I hated how fate seemed to crap on me every chance it got. Pretty soon I was going to have to kick its butt, but how? How do you do that when everything feels against you, everyone around you is a poor example of how to live your life and fierce rebellion is boiling through your veins trying to get out? What can make the difference in a life gone wrong? I didn't appreciate the good thing that I had and now it was gone. What was I missing? I was sick of this feeling of impending doom and watching destruction play out in my life. There are eight cousins in my family and everybody has this cloud over them. It is killing us in so many ways, how can we stop it?

Chapter 11 - Natural Bridge
Marcus

One of my cousins came out to visit and stayed at our house until my dad kicked him out. He moved down by the beach and went crazy. We think he got some bad PCP. He's on disability now. Most of my cousins had it rough, some did prison time, and many were abused or abandoned altogether. Many sold drugs and got busted, one was in a national drug ring, with health benefits and everything. Not really. His brother did ten years in prison though. They were supposed to be this huge rap conglomerate, but it was a cover. His parents basically abandoned him once he stopped listening. If you leave your kids alone or push them out, they may make poor choices and they will hate you. Then they will make it your fault. Truth! Aunts and Uncles doing drugs, what a dysfunctional bunch we are! Not much for role models, right? Kids need role models.

I had Mr. Breland, my football coach and neighbor, who took an interest in me and was a type of surrogate father. He was kind to me, his son was my age and he saw something in me. Never underestimate the difference you can make in a kids life just by being kind. Sometimes I think our kid's friends are an opportunity for us to teach our kids indirectly and be someone for them, too. We all need someone to care about us. Especially kids with no father. Greg Wade was my best friend and an incredible break dancer. He was a humble light-skinned black guy who was lovable and took a liking to me. His Mom was cool, and loved the Lord, but this Jesus thing was weird to me. Then during the summer I stayed in Virginia and hung out with the Greg's family a lot, they were great and showed me what a real family could be like. They were not rich, but it didn't matter. They were solid and loved me like one of the family. I started stealing bikes and selling them to get back at Herb. I did not want anything from him, especially his money. I was trying to get back at him, but I was only hurting myself. I hid the bikes at Greg's house in the country. I would go down to the beach and bring them back, easy money baby! I went to church one time with the Wade's. It was the

African Episcopal Methodist church. I never saw anything like that before. The people there were jumping up and kissing the Holy Spirit. They were banging on drums and on the tables, dancing around, it was like the circus or something. What a scene! Herb was mad about me going to church. Greg's mom called Herb one day to pick me up for my court appearance, which I was trying to avoid. He came to their house and Herb then threw me in trunk of his company car. Nobody said a word.

I was tired of being treated like a dog. I had created success at school and had learned how to play the game pretty well, but I would still run away to avoid my dad. Then he would look for me, to find me, to afflict me and to bring me back. By now, he had a mail order business in our garage. He also learned how to record and tap our phone conversations. It was hard to get around him. I learned computers early for Herb's mail order business. More technology, more strange behavior from Herb. I passed eighth grade and Herb wanted to hold me back to punish me, I hated him more and spent much of my ninth grade year in detention homes since I was hanging out with the bad kids, breaking into cars, stealing stuff and all to avoid my dad. I even put a smoke bomb in the industrial arts cabinet at school and got to spend two months at a mental health center before I could return to school. With all the kerosene and stuff in there, it's a wonder I didn't blow up the half the school. Herb and I probably could have settled a lot of it with a ten minute conversation, but we never had it. No one tried to find out the why behind what I was doing. Sometimes I think we're too afraid to get into someone's personal life and that's too bad. A lot of times we feel drawn toward someone because we can help them. We may not understand it all yet, but we can help them. When that feeling is present, it's not to be ignored. Lives are messy, but to make a difference, we have to get in there and help, just meet people where they're at. It may be just a kind word, a smile or it may be years of companionship, the point is to get involved. Hours we spend watching TV may be better spent doing art, walking or making new friends. Give it a try.

I didn't care what happened to me, I just needed to be apart from Herb. I attacked him once. He hit me so hard, I never tried again. I lived in fear of him every moment. The beatings were common and never corrective, they were just brutality now. I was scared of my father. Nothing had changed. My sister was still being molested. One time I was trying to hide from Herb and he saw me behind a fence with my friends. He was so mad, he beat me with a fence board in front of my cool friends with my pants down. Then he humiliated me and made me say something. He said, "Tell them, you're not the man! Say it!" He prodded me and I did. I could have gutted him on the spot and fed him to the birds. No one should do that to a kid. You become the biggest laughingstock. The kids at school hammered me over that one and I fought a lot over it.

I had to pass a summer Geometry class so I could take advanced math and Herb was committed to it. He cleared out the furniture and put a desk in for me to finish my Geometry class. Then came the worst thing yet. He had a big trash can that he filled with concrete. Then he ran three chains into the concrete. One for my legs, one for my arms and one for my waist. This dude was sick and he put a big padlock on it so I would stay there. He put it around me and attached it to me tightly like I was a dog or something to keep me from running away again. He premeditated my torture and made it himself, put in right there in the front room. My Mom, my sisters all saw it, and said nothing out of fear. Hey man, you really are fucking crazy! I knew it for sure in this moment. Herb was gone off the deep end. Herb created a prison for me and he chained me to it, so I would have to stay home and not move. This dude was whacked out completely. Although I love her deeply, I still have hard feelings toward Mom over it all. He left me there all day and she let him do it. It was abnormal, total tyranny and I hated her so much for letting him do it! One day after spending lots of time trying to get out, I finally was able to break one of the links of the dog chain and get away from the trash can and the house of horrors. I went to the mall with the chain on me and found Greg, who took me to his house and we got the chain off of me. I went bonkers, I stole Herbs car and I wrecked it. Out of control, I hit a telephone pole and I could have died. The seatbelt kept me in. I was reacting to his malice and evil intent.

My hatred was renewed at higher, deeper and darker levels. My psyche was feeling fragile. Just another day with Herb and Mom in a life gone wrong. I was so young and felt so weak, so broken, and ready to kill him. My hope was gone. I didn't care about anything anymore except getting away from him. The walls and the law were closing in on me. I was a volcano ready to burst. I wasn't the problem. How come there are no programs for parents in trouble? I loved nature and in this place, the Natural Bridge Juvenile Detention Center, I could see yet another world. The pain and the angst inside people causes them to be broken, lonely and horrific to each other. It has played out in both our lives so many times. There is a well inside every heart and whatever you fill it with is whatever will flow out of it. Think garbage in, garbage out. What we would like to see rather is a whole new focus and way of thinking: treasure in, treasure out. Our country is dying for a lack of hope anymore. People don't care about each other like they once did. At least it seems that way. There's not always a community spirit, like barn raising in the old days for example, when the whole town would gather and help someone put up their barn. It was helpful and it was necessary to get it done. No one could do it by themselves. Our communities have to become this again. Willing to share and help each other. It's not simple or easy, but it's needed.

We have to get wiser and understand we can effect very little beyond our attitudes. It's up to us to navigate the rapids of life but we cannot build the river. We don't have to like everything, but we can see the good in it, if we choose to. It's a choice. Just a year ago my uncle Frankie broke the trash can up. Can you imagine? It sat around that house for almost thirty freaking years. "You're free", he said. Surprisingly, something did break off of me, years of garbage were released and I found some new hope in that moment. My Mom just sold that old house and it also felt like something got off my back in that, too. It's funny how long those things can be attached to you. There are things that have to be broken off and we're going to teach you some ways to do that later on. To break free yes, but also to stay free.

The only way I knew to fight back was by acting out. I smoked, drank, got in fights, shoplifted, stole bikes and hung out 24-7. I had no real home, just my friends who were more like my family now. Social services would come out because my sister would call them about the abuse and they would do nothing to help us. They just left us there, oh my God! Abuse piling up and they just walked away. Eventually all the running away, curfew violations and breaking into abandon houses to stay, led me to the woods. I wanted to be someone else, so I was acting it out all the time. I had to survive, but I needed help. The law caught up to me and I spent my tenth grade year in a juvenile facility called Natural Bridge Camp for Boys. It was a boy's home and another chance to fix what was wrong with me. I was honestly getting tired of everyone thinking that it was me that was the problem. It is a part of the Youth Conservation Corps now. It's a 1600 acre property nestled in the heart of the forest. Mr. Aristotle was my history teacher and he made things come alive. I met Mr. Redd, my counselor. He was from Roanoke and he knew there was something more in me. We shared music and I learned to trust him.

They created an environment where I could respect myself, where I could learn from others. It was important to be a part of the group and to learn by doing. Many people forget how men need to do that. They need the interaction, they need to learn by doing. They taught me better study habits. I was always on cruise control with school. I had to learn to work hard, not just be smart and get by. It has served me well. So has learning respect, discipline and wisdom. The problem was, ever since St. Louis, I wanted to kill Herb, so while I loved what they taught me, I also had a huge obstacle to overcome. The risky behavior was off the charts, everything Herb did now was to ridicule and belittle me. I responded by being an out of control risk taker with no sense of morals or purpose. I was headed to prison or the morgue. Everybody liked me, but not my step dad. A tough road to navigate.

In the Blue Ridge Mountains I found myself a little. I think I was becoming institutionalized from what was happening to me. I needed to breathe. I learned Lacrosse and got good at football. There was a Chinese guy who used a type of music therapy on me and made me learn how to relax. I became a music lover of all styles. I didn't want to go home anymore. I was afraid for my sisters, but I just had to get free from my family. The staff would ask, "Why do you get in trouble?" They were kind to me, they made me trust them and told me they would help me. They were always keeping their word and making me accountable. Even the punishment was helpful because they made me see consequences for my actions, but they did it with respect, not tyranny or force. It brought out the best in me, but it scared the hell out of me, too. I was teetering on the edge and then I confessed it to them. They broke me down. Not all of it, but enough of what had happened with my stepdad. The rush of emotion that came out of me was scary and difficult to stop. I was out of control again. I just told someone my deepest, darkest secret. Was I out of my mind? Fear and anxiety crashed over me like relentless waves off Oahu.

Then came the conference with the staff and Herb. They confronted him. He cried about it and confessed his mistakes and promised to be better. He even hugged me and told me that he was sorry for the first time in my life. It was very convincing to the staff, but it was a lie. I hope that someday he will see his mistakes and admit them. It would bring him the freedom he never had. For all the scars he left me, I still want to see him get free. It took a long time to see him as a person, but eventually I did and I know he went through a lot to become the man who I knew. He just never did the work to get free or get better. It's the hard part and some people won't go there and do it no matter what. I hope that you do it if you need to. One good thing I take away from him was when we would listen to all kinds of music together. He hated us to use his turntable and play albums. He was afraid we would scratch them. He had great taste and had an interesting variety of artists like Johnny Mathis and Miles Davis. Overall, I'm disgusted because he could have gotten help with his stuff and been a different person. At least I understand it some now. It's hard to forgive him. You don't know how messed up you are sometimes. It's tough when you have to disown your own family to at least to have a chance to survive. How do you repair yourself or your kids? Is it even possible? It's a question we have asked ourselves for a long time. We're still asking it today. So much to learn and know. There's so much to overcome and grow from. Sounds like a great opportunity, if you think about it for a while.

Chapter 12 – Girls
Marcus

After Natural Bridge I was a different person and I came home. There were over 5000 kids at Green Run High School and I was one of them. I had been going to institutional high school and now I was in the big time. I tried out for the football team and I made it! They had a Mr. Green Run Beauty Pageant and I finished 4th among the men. That got me a lot of attention! It was nice to be noticed for something good for a change! Girls like a trophy man! I was with my neighborhood sweetheart, she was a pretty white girl and I caught serious flack for that. I got it from the black girls at school, my family and Herb the racist. Her parents did not like black people either. We could talk at school, but not at home. More of the double life. I became two different people, one at school and one at home. I had friends who were hanging out with me and protecting me, even feeding me. I really liked this girl, she seemed to understand things without being told all the time. She was helping me more than I thought, even though her family didn't like me that much. They tolerated me because we were neighbors. We were boyfriend and girlfriend at school and casual friends at home. I wonder what they would have thought if they had known the truth. I was very confident. I started believing things could be good. At school I was friends with everyone. It was crazy. Herb was even acting better towards me. He was still molesting my sister and I just stayed away from home as much as I could. My neighbor and I got closer. She was mad at her dad for cheating on her mom while he was stationed up north in the service. Green Run High School had some pretty amazing athletes who played football. I was getting pretty good, I went to camps and Mr. Breland thought I could play college ball. I was a tall, fast wide receiver and I went to visit Charlottesville, home of the University of Virginia. It was never on my radar before, but I had a chance now. A ton of professional athletes went there and maybe I had a chance to go, too. Anything seemed possible for me.

As life and times progressed with my neighbor, we were very close and she got pregnant during the middle of my senior year of high school. Life took a new twist. Her parents were not thrilled and we had no way to support a baby. So even though college and a future were on the horizon, I chose to quit going to high school during senior year and got my GED instead. I was trying to be a good guy and take care of things like a real man should. The goal was to marry her and join the service. I went to the recruiter and I tested out as an Air Traffic controller. What a great career opportunity! Then before I was supposed to join, I was in a major car accident. A drunk driver hit me head on. He broke my foot in eight places, my jaw was wired shut and I was in a coma for three days. My injuries were very serious and the military was out of the question now. This was more evidence of how life seemed to work. Always something to screw it up. So here I am with limited education, a baby on the way, a struggling marriage and I'm 18 years old. I knew nothing about what a good father does and I had no direction in what to do with my life. It was a mess, but this one I made myself. Every door seemed to be closing. When you know life as being dysfunctional and that's the only thing you know, it's easy to stay there. So the at-risk boy became the at-risk adult. I never understood why trying to do the right thing almost got me killed. Herb settled the lawsuit with the insurance company from the car accident and kept my money. I needed it, but he had a way of screwing everything up, even my way out. He was a pro at making life a freak show!

There is no way anyone could make up for all the damage. If I stay in that place where I feel sorry for myself, focus on the circumstances and blame everyone else for my problems, I will never get free. I could focus on the pain or I could decide to forgive my parents, not to let them off the hook, but to take the hook out of my heart. There is purpose in everything in life, even the trauma, even the sadness and pain. Bad things happen, but it's what we do with them that matters. This life is never easy, it's a crap pile somedays and the Academy Awards on others. The trick is to keep your perspective. Don't get too high or too low. Work hard, save money, do good, make a difference and keep your eyes open. Don't be afraid to change or love with your whole heart.

Everyone will have struggles at times, but they are much better stories than they are descriptions of who you are now. Victims die, overcomers conquer and that's what we want to be. Your circumstances reveal your identity, they don't define it. Pressure comes to bring forth the diamonds, not to tell the coal it is a dirty lump of carbon.

Chapter 13 – Graduation
Rick

So after all the mess of wrecking the car, life settled down again. I was playing baseball and I was the top seller for our fundraising project. We sold sausage and snacks, cheese and t-shirts. It was easy. People seemed to like me again. I wanted to do well. Mom was settling down again. She met an ex-marine, Jerry and he was a piece of work, too. He had a twinkle in his eye and he made her behave, which was unique. They met in a bar. I know, shocking. Before my senior year, Jerry moved in with us. He was a decent guy, maybe a little full of himself. But he had a way of talking that made me believe in possibilities. He spoke of climbing mountains and how good life could be, once you figured it out. I appreciated his idea of fun because anything was better than hanging around the asylum all day.

I'm amazed how many times, with all the different stepfathers and people in and out of my life, each brought something I needed. I remember after Don and before Jerry, there was this guy Gene. He came in our front door with a bottle of vodka and a case of Budweiser and I thought, "Who's this asshole?" I was about sixteen. There were three stepdads that year alone. Gene was arrogant, smelly, everything I hated, but he brought me a great gift. He had a son about my age and I had always wanted a brother close to my own age. The son was funny and a lot like me. Obviously he shared and understood the sheer goofiness of the world I lived in, without saying a word. We just knew. It was really refreshing for a couple of months. It helped me be able to have confidence at the new school I was going to and just feel comfortable in my own skin for a change. I always felt like the weird kid. I had a fear if I told anybody anything, they would use it against me to hate me or mock me. So I built a great wall with a high tower to protect myself. My place of security was also my prison in time. Men are often getting away or running away. Sometimes they are staying in the prison they made to protect themselves. *Thanks Geno for being my friend, my brother and someone to share it with. You made a difference in me. I hope it's going well for you!*

We had a cat. He was a stray and his name was Barracuda. He was black, cool and sleek and we played football together. Well, sort of. I had a Nerf football that I would throw in his general direction and he would shred carpet running away. I used to chase him around and it was great fun. We had a long hallway with a pass-through kitchen so we could do the loop together. One day I walked into the living room and I said, "Hello kitty." He looked at me, jumped straight up in the air, about four feet, spun around in midair and landed with legs pumping. He left a lot of carpet in his wake. It was so funny, I almost fell over. He was so cool and fun. I feel bad because I probably whacked him out. One day he jumped onto the kitchen window ledge. I couldn't open the screen without knocking him off so I got on the porch railing three stories up and tried to reach him. He backed up into a tiny ball and I couldn't reach him. So I put my life at risk and balanced on one foot and reached over and grabbed one paw. He was pissed, but when I brought him into the apartment safely, he was very grateful. It was really stupid to do that. In hindsight, I should have cut the screen. My angels were watching over me that day!

So Mom and Jerry decided to get married. It would be a small wedding, but weddings are cool. She asked me to give her away. I wonder how many times I wanted to do that over the years. We had started to become close for the first time. I saw her as a person, she saw me as a good helper. Well, except for the day when she fried up six leg-thigh quarters of chicken. I was really hungry so I ate, and ate, and ate. Pretty soon, the whole plate was gone. When I told her that I had eaten it all, she didn't believe me. She thought it took several friends to eat that much food. I laughed and said, "What's for dinner?" She finally smiled and her path to healing was near. It may take years to get over the trauma. Laughter is the accelerant to get you there. Take it out for a spin. It works, if you let it.

The sexual abuse stayed with her most of her life. She never found a way out of the pain and she felt dirty and worthless. I'm sure somehow she thought it was her fault. I guess that's why she went to the bars so often looking for a version of herself that she never found. She needed help, but didn't know where to begin. That's true for most of us. Where do we go to start to unravel the mess? Sometimes it's as simple as getting a good counselor. A good counselor is someone you can trust. If you meet with someone and it doesn't feel right, you can try someone else. It may take a few, but keep at it, it's worth the healing to keep looking. I had a friend once who found a great counselor and she made an impact, but she was expensive. My friend started doing odd jobs, painting houses, whatever it took to get the money to see this lady. It was true transformation. It's wonderful to find someone like that. They're out there, sometimes you have to look for a while to find them. I was determined never to be my Mom and to do whatever it took to be free. It's not easy, but it is so worth it.

That's a big part of the reason I am writing this book, so that others can know: there is hope and it can be good. No matter what has happened in life, you, too, can be set free. You have to want to be different and you probably have to have help to get there. Don't carry it around forever. You can be free, your life can be transformed and it can be incredible, more than you ever imagined. Yes, it is possible. Maybe you weren't born free but you can be made free. It's all about having the courage to go back and deal with whatever messed you up, for as long as it takes.

Chapter 14 - Pekoe by Rick E. Roberts (5-13-16)

Pekoe was the smallest warrior of his tribe. He knew Mammy and Pappy loved him. He was shorter than most for his age, but he loved being part of a family. There were many other tribes in the area to meet and share things with. He liked the Redlanders best because they always had little pieces of hard candy that they made by hand, and they were really good at sharing them! There were the Massaqua and the Otters who made beautiful clothes and sometimes he would even see the Sempers. They didn't come around very often, but more than the Wolves did. He heard a lot of interesting stories about the Wolves. They didn't sound nice. They were always taking things from the other tribes and generally being difficult. Their aggression was in contrast to most of the tribal families who had learned how to get along with each other. They knew how to share and help each other. Not the Wolves.

Pappy sat down to tell Pekoe a story. "Come here Pekoe, and hear the tale I want to tell," Pappy said. "The Wolves have a problem with our tribe, the Ravens, because of something that happened many moons ago. Our ancient Chief Thunder Hawk offered to help the Wolves with food when they were hungry after a crop failure. So we loaded a small wagon full of bread, grain and jerky, corn and rice and sent out two braves to take it there. It started raining, but they were committed to getting the food there quickly. Maybe a little too quickly. As the horses pulled the wagon there was a spot by the creek where the road was slippery. Before they knew it, the wagon slid off the road. The horses tried to pull it out with no luck. When they unhooked the horses, the wagon fell into the creek. The water rose fast and they rode off to tell the Wolves what happened. Two of the Wolves rode back with them to see the wagon and try to get it out. The rain was pounding now and the creek rose so much and so fast that the wagon was completely covered in water. They came upon where they thought it was and they looked, but couldn't find it. The Wolves started yelling at the Ravens, accusing them of lying. The Ravens braves got angry and a fight ensued. The two tribes were not friends anymore. The Wolves moved farther out, distancing themselves from the other tribes, they felt betrayed and unloved. The truth was the Ravens had tried to help. Unfortunately it didn't work out. The tribes separated from each other, but I believe, someday they will come back together. As sure as the sun will rise in the East. What do you think Pekoe?" Pappy said.

"That's a good story Pappy, can you show me the place where it happened?" he asked. "I will try Pekoe, but only the Great Spirit knows for sure," said Pappy. Pekoe thought long and hard about the story. It made him sad that the tribes were divided now. He thought maybe it was time to change that, but how? Later that week Pappy said, "Get your horse Pekoe, we will ride out to the spot and see if we can find it. It's just past the bend in the river." "Okay Pappy," said Pekoe. They rode together in silence for a long time and finally Pappy said, "Look! I see some horse prints, but they don't look like our horses, the hooves are bigger." Who could it be?

Pekoe looked around and thought he saw a tiny bit of color behind a tree. Just then a bear came out from behind the tree and frightened the horses. Pappy's horse reared up and he fell right off the saddle onto the ground. The bear stood up on its back legs and it was a large Grizzly. Pekoe was terrified, he wanted to help Pappy, but he was frozen in fear. Every bit of his being was overwhelmed. Pappy was laying there helpless. His leg was badly hurt, maybe even broken. The bear headed his way in fury. Just then a large warrior came out from behind the tree. The bear roared and charged. The Warrior got between the bear and Pappy. He fired his first arrow and pierced the bear. This only made him angrier. The warrior set up to fire again, but the bear had gotten to him and took a swipe at his head, just missing. The warrior ran and Pappy was left alone. The bear turned his gaze and ferocity on Pappy now. Pekoe let out a high pitched squeak and the bear turned to see him, still frozen in place. This distraction allowed the warrior to sneak up on the bear and pierce him with a long spear. The weapon ripped into the bear's flesh. This time the bear ran at the warrior and he didn't miss, taking a piece of flesh out of his leg and the blood flowed freely. The pandemonium was escalating. Something happened inside Pekoe, instead of being filled with fear, he suddenly had a peace come upon him. He

92

was still terrified but he was off his horse and running toward the bear. The warrior backed up and hit the bear again with a second arrow. Pekoe grabbed a rock. It looked bigger than he was. He tried to throw it at the bear, but he dropped it. The bear came at him on all fours and it looked like the end. Pekoe picked up the rock again and dropped it on the bear. It hit him right on the nose. In his bloody and dazed state, the bear didn't see the warrior coming up behind him. Pappy had scooted himself to his bow and shot an arrow right into the bear's leg and the warrior thrust his spear deep into his side. There was a lot of blood everywhere. The bear lashed out and roared, he was wounded badly. Pekoe ran to Pappy to try to get him on his feet again. The warrior went towards the bear, but the bear had had enough. He staggered away with a mighty roar. The sound of it froze all three of them for a moment, stopping time.

The warrior watched the bear stagger off and then watched Pappy and Pekoe for a long time. He then came over and spoke, "You are very brave young one. You must be the beloved son to have such courage. I saw you frozen in fear and something changed in you. What was it?" Pekoe looked at him carefully. He was very kind, but he looked like one of the Wolves. Hesitantly he said, "I knew nothing bad could happen as long as Pappy was with me. Can I help with your wound?" Pekoe was a very good medicine man. He had his bag full of powder, clean cloth and spices. The warrior nodded yes. Pekoe felt like he had to ask, "Are you one of the Wolves?"

The warrior nodded again and then let out a stifled yell as Pekoe applied spices and the first cloth over his leg. The blood started coagulating nicely. Pekoe finished binding his wounds and turned his attention to Pappy. The leg wasn't broken, but Pekoe wrapped it tightly with a branch so he could put a little weight on it. The horses had returned and were thirsty and anxious from the bear attack.

The three of them walked the horses down toward the creek. Pappy had to stop and sit so he gave his horse to Pekoe. They walked to the water and what they saw next was unexpected. The warrior helped Pekoe navigate the bank once his horse was drinking. Just then Pekoe saw it. Part of a wagon wheel between the rocks. Could it be? He called after Pappy. "Is this the spot?" He said. "Look for our tribal mark on the lazy back seat." Pekoe walked on a rock and then went into the river. He walked right up and there it was. "Is this the wagon Pappy?" "I think it is Pekoe, from so long ago," said Pappy. The emblem was faded, but there, so well-hidden for many years.

He turned to the warrior and said, "Do you know the story?" The warrior said, "Yes, my Pappy was one of the two braves who came out to see the wagon, but it wasn't there." Pekoe felt suddenly bold. He went under water, reached into the wagon and he found a bag of corn. It was old, but it was corn. He had found the wagon. "What should we do?" He said. The warrior looked at him with a tear in his eye and said, "Pekoe, you have restored our tribes today because you know who you are. You are mighty in words, actions and deeds. You will need to teach my tribe this way. They have become suspicious, nasty and foolish because we have forgotten who we are. I was scouting your tribe to see what I could steal. I am sorry. It is time to change our ways, please forgive us. The Great Spirit had to bring the bear into our lives to wound us so we could turn to Him. Thank you for opening my eyes to the truth." Pekoe didn't know what to say. Pappy looked and him and said, "You are my beloved son, Pekoe. In you I am well pleased. You overcame your fear and defeated the enemy bear with your love, strength and self-sacrifice. You saved me Pekoe. You saved us all."

The warrior spoke after a long pause, "Shiki," (which means friend). He said turning to Pappy, "I remember your kindness to my grandfather. He spoke of you often in private. He told me stories about the adventures you shared on the river and by the waterfall, long before the wagon separated us. He even told me about the girl you both liked, how she became your wife!" They all laughed. Pekoe smiled and shook his head, "Mammy," he said. The warrior continued, "That's why I stepped in to help you, you are a good man and I admire you. You have done well with Pekoe and I honor you. You have been faithful to helping him and I believe he will finish well."

Then Pappy looked at him with a smile and extended his hand to shake it. He said, "You are a beloved son, too. Your grandfather would be very proud. You have become a mighty warrior, worthy of honor and high ranking in your tribe. All the deeds of the past have been forgiven and washed away. Your courage has saved your tribe and ours. Come to our camp for tonight and tomorrow we will go to see your tribe together and tell them the story. Then we can all be one again." Pekoe looked on with wonder at all that had taken place. His heart was full of joy. The Wolves and the Ravens could be brothers again. All because he knew who he was and who he belonged to. Unity came back to the tribes that day. The three of them rode off together towards a brave new future. It was still uncertain, but it was certain to be together.

Chapter 15 - Georgetown or Bust
Marcus

I tried to do the right thing by my new wife. We were so young and we fought verbally and sometimes physically. We apologized to each other, but every fight pulled us apart. I hated that I was becoming my father. After all the drama we moved to Washington, DC. It was a fresh start away from our cheating dads.

I was healed from the car accident and my first real job was at the Arlington Employment Commission. This is where I learned how important jobs are. My wife and I needed each other. Everyone needs love. We cared about each other, but I don't think we were built to last. We were immature, naive and ready to go on an amazing adventure. Our son is a beautiful little man. We were definitely a work in progress. Her parents took our son for a while so we could work out our relationship and try to get settled in.

We were at a bus station. We could have stayed with my cousin, but we decided we would get a motel room on the Arlington Highway. This highway is really a heavy place for drugs and sex trafficking. We didn't know. This was long before the review sites and hotel apps we have today. We were waiting for the hotel person and we met this guy Scott who invited us into his room. He was pimping hookers right there in the motel. They kept us captive in that room for hours. He wanted my wife to do hooking and for me to be okay with it. He gave us drugs and a lot of drinks. We were young people from Virginia Beach hanging out with expert freaks. We were the most naïve motherfuckers ever. They were trolling for people to use. Finally I got to a phone and was able to call 911. The police came and got us out of there and took us to the homeless shelter. It was so freaky!

Our relationship got worse. We got our son back when we moved into our own apartment. We got work at The Nature Conservatory and found a really cool new thing: happy hour! What could be cooler than cheap drinks and free food? It was a tough time. Our son was moved around as we tried to make it work. She was going to stay with me and try one more time, but her family convinced her to move to out. My heart was broken. She moved to her Grandma's place in Indiana. Sometimes I wonder if she hooked up with me to teach her parents a lesson. Was I teaching my family a lesson? Maybe she was told that black people were animals, just like Herb told me about whites. Maybe she realized they weren't, just like I did. Why do parents fill us with hate and lies so often? What is missing or messed up in them that they promote hate like it's valuable. We have a long way to go as people.

I knew bad stuff was still going on at my old house and that wasn't the right place for me to stay. I got my stuff and I didn't see my Mom for a year after that. I couldn't let them hurt me anymore. With my wife and child leaving me, wow, I was just so hurt and lost. I still feared my father and I just did not want to be in Virginia Beach anymore, ever. I had cheated on my wife. She had cheated on me. I started dating another woman at work and that became very messy. I was trying to keep it together. Trying to learn how to be a good role model, a decent parent and a stand-up guy was too much. Trying to learn on the fly with no back ground was ridiculous. Trying to learn with Herb's example was impossible. She wanted to move back to Virginia Beach and I didn't, so I stayed in DC.

I was hard-working and I was dating chicks all over, nursing my pain. DC is a place where it's like four women to one guy ratio and I was a single guy and so naïve. I had gotten this great job at the Nature Conservancy making $26,000 with my own office. I thought I was hot stuff. I went to this conference and I met a guy from Montana. He talked about an internship to work out there. Hmmm? I started hanging out with cultured women and learning what salad forks were for and what wines were good. I had so much to learn. The end was clearly upon us. Work became everything. I loved the non-profit culture because it was doing something with a purpose. I still work in non-profits to this day. It's what I was born for. I was on my own as a divorced father with no clue how to navigate life at all.

My sister, Zhalih continued to have major liver problems that required lengthy hospital stays. She had cirrhosis of the liver, but she never drank alcohol. She was tired of the physical abuse from Herb and moved to Washington, DC, too. Herb used to leave money for her after he abused her sexually. Hundred dollar bills he would throw on the floor, I guess it was hush money. Imagine your father a serial rapist and you're the victim. Makes me wanna holler! She saved it so she could get away. Hell must have a special place for fathers like that. Zhalih had kept a journal of what happened to her. That turned out to be very important later on.

Life became a bottomless system of money, drinking and partying. I thought I was so cosmopolitan. I spent a lot of time in the bars and I had a bad habit of getting into fights because someone would bump into me and I would explode and start fighting. I learned it long ago and my friends would be like, "Why do you do that Marcus?" I was defending my turf, don't touch me! You can't be weak or tolerate anyone disrespecting you. That much I knew. All it really proved was how far I still had to go. I was processing pain. I felt like a failure, not just a product of my environment anymore. These choices were mine. I was still the at-risk adult. I never knew what limitations were for and it would come back to haunt me time and time again. I was lost and alone, immature and broken. I needed help but I was good at hiding it. It was only getting worse.

Chapter 16 – Mines
Rick

So I got the coolest job ever after high school. I went to work at Elitch's, an amusement park in Denver. It was a place to goof off and get paid. I enjoyed running the kitchen and setting sail on the next part of my adventure. I was really excited for the free admission, cheap food and cute girls from all over town. I graduated high school, but I didn't know what I wanted to do. I thought about going to college and staying in state would be much cheaper. I had a few hundred letters from colleges. No one offered me a scholarship, but I had an unlikely advocate on my side.

During the winter, Jerry #2 went with me to talk to the financial aid guy at the Colorado School of Mines. I was excited about science and math. I took the ACT test and did very well. I placed in the top 7% in science in the country and the top 12% in math. Those two scores played in my favor as did my Mom's financial situation. Everything worked together for my good and I was offered a full tuition scholarship to one of the finest engineering schools in the world. Everything in life was setting up to be the redemption I had been waiting for. Finally the dream was coming true! Thanks to Mr. Young for believing in me and helping me get financial aid! It was my road to success time.

We had a tradition that all incoming freshmen would hike up a mountain and whitewash a giant M that was on Mount Zion, just outside the campus boundaries. Joe O'Bryne, head of the Mines Department of Descriptive Geometry, laid it out on the mountain in 1905. It was hundreds of rocks and was added to and improved upon over the years. In 1932 permanent electric lighting was added. The dimensions are 104' by 107' and is the world's largest electrically lit school emblem. I missed the whitewash, made the varsity baseball team and I registered for 19 credit hours to start off with a bang! Little did I realize that this was no joke. University courses at the best engineering school in the country is a fourteen hour a day commitment or more. Rude awakening time! I had a lot of challenges to overcome and school on steroids was not helping. I kept struggling to catch up.

There were very few girls who went there, but a few in my classes were cute so I had to find time for them, too! I wanted to be something and I was drowning in a sea of equations, formulas, homework and processing my junk. It looked great on the outside, as it usually did, but inside was a disaster. That year my Grandma was visiting for Christmas when my grades came in the mail. I'll never forget coming home and discovering she had opened them already. I was pissed. She had no right! The story it told was a horror movie. Not only did I struggle, but I was placed on academic suspension. I couldn't even go to school the next semester, I had to sit out. Goodbye scholarship, hello mediocrity! Life came to a screaming halt. What was I going to do now? I went and talked to one of my friends, he said the I-Club was hiring for a cook on campus. I could stay on campus and get my head on straight and start again. The job was fine, short order cook for students, one man kitchen, serving beer, easy clean up. Pay was okay, got to see a lot of my friends and meet the upperclassmen. Maybe I still had a chance? Baseball was out and that really bugged me. I was pitching in college as a freshmen and now I was on the bench. Marv Kay was a great coach and he told me to hang in there. Life bit me on the butt and now I had to fix it, again.

I remember a beautiful girl from Michigan. She was the cutest girl at Mines and while I was working in the cafe, I was friendly to her friend, so the pressure was off. Then I asked her friend to ask her if she liked me. She did and it was a dream come true. She was an upperclassmen and beautiful inside and out. She had a great body and a 3.2 GPA. She was going to be a good wage earner and fun to be with. Something started to make sense in my mind for us. Our first date was splendid! Great conversation and food. I started to believe. Then we went back to her place! Say no more, but I will. We got going hot and heavy and she finally said, "Wait, we've got to slow down." We were going to do it right there. I really liked her, I admired her and I respected her. I didn't push anything even though we wanted each other desperately. She seemed to take it personally, like I was trying to be a creep or get the milk for free. I wasn't just in heat over her. I'm not a one night cowboy! I really liked her! At that point, I even needed her! She made me believe in miracles, but something happened in her heart and she stopped coming around the I-Club. It got to be a very lonely place for me. I started drinking beer when I was there to numb the pain. I felt like such a loser, I lost my scholarship and now I lost her. What an idiot I was! I was trying to turn over a new leaf, but it was turning me over and kicking my ass, too! Failure came for another visit, what a pest it was becoming.

After a couple of months, they asked me to clean the floors in the cafeteria kitchen at night after I finished downstairs. It was a mess, they made all the pastry by hand and the slobs trashed the place. I lasted maybe a week, I hated it. I met a guy Rob Randall who took my place, he was a really nice guy. He was so happy for the job and he took it seriously. I got to be good friends with him. He was on the six year plan, he went to school and worked, too. Very few people finished Mines in four years, it was all consuming. He had a poor financial background like me. I was really excited for him, he was almost finished. About two months later, he got his degree in petroleum engineering. Happy days are here again! Later I heard he was working on an oil platform down in Louisiana, his first job and he was making great money! Something happened when the sea shifted and he fell off the rig and died instantly. I was so pissed off when I heard it, I could have bit through steel. He worked so hard for so long and overcame so much. Damn it! I hated how our stories turned out this way! Starting with two strikes against you sucked and now he was dead. Stupid freaking life! He had the same background as me and he almost made it. It stole some of my joy. It still does.

As I was working there, I became friends with Eric, who worked in the bowling alley. One night he came in and stole a keg. Since I was there, they blamed me for it. I went to city jail, got a citation and had to pay a fine. Another brick in the wall of shame. Then I met a group of guys at Mines who were big time partiers. They became my next group of freaks to hang with. They had an engineered bong called the Baffler. It was designed to cool the smoke as it passed through ice and baffles, it was ahead of its time, smooth as silk. Their version of college was to screw off all semester and cram like maniacs for the last two days. Greg had a 3.3 GPA one semester doing that. Now college was permanently

103

tainted. What was I going to do now? I couldn't go back to Mines with that charge on my record. When were the clouds going to break?

Chapter 17 - Big Hank
Marcus

I was officially invited to take the paid internship to Montana with The Nature Conservancy and after two minutes of pondering I was off! That decision was life changing. We put up trail signs and flora and fauna identifying signs on trails. It was great fun. My love of the outdoors was rekindled. I was there by myself at first. My job was unique. We were way out West so they gave me a car and everything I needed. I was in Helena, Montana, that's a long way from the east coast and Herb and the drama. I could breathe, it felt like I hit the reset button. I lived in the country and I worked in the city and then I would go out to different trails which were far away. Nothing was close by. We had a dude ranch to work at, too. I actually learned how to ride horses! It was the hardest soil ever. Hard work and calluses, sometimes they're a good thing. When I was in Montana I won a tight fitting jeans contest. During that time, I came up with the moniker Big Hank, which is my karaoke stage name. I walked into a country bar called the Silver Spur and I was the only black guy there, maybe in all of Montana! Just as I walked in, the music stopped and everybody stared at me. Montana could be a racist place, but once you were around for a while, they gave you a pass.

The Nature Conservancy's goal was protecting land from development. I was surprised how so many of the Native Americans were hard drinkers and drunks. They had no hope and it made me sad. I had not met one before and I didn't know how to reach them. One day there were two bears on the trail I was on. There was something good about the west. I was still always on guard, even with Herb 2500 miles away. Some things don't go away easily. I got a ticket for mouthing off to the cops one night and of course, it was in the newspaper the next day. I spent the night in jail for my big mouth. Montana was a funky place, it was snowing in the summer and I liked the wide open spaces. It got me thinking and breathing in a new way. Big skies do a heart good sometimes.

After the internship, I went back to Virginia Beach to try to get back with my wife and be close to Mom and my sisters. It didn't work out. I was still out of control sometimes. I would hang out with my friends after work and still get into fights. They were like, "We just want to get a bite to eat. You just don't pop people for stuff like that." I still didn't know any different. When I came back I had changed and the world looked different for me. I decided to move to Denver and wanted to work for the Nature Conservancy there. I wanted to get as far away from Herb as possible. He was going through a public molestation trial and wearing an ankle monitor. He not only molested my sister, but my girlfriend at the time and even my wife for a short period. It was painful to hear all this. He, eventually, went to prison for all of his perversion. Good riddance! I got my dad's tools and got me some get back with him. I took his tools to the pawnshop. Yes, all of them! I wanted to take everything and it was payback for my insurance money. It felt good to screw him over for once. Real good!

Chapter 18 - Free Delivery
Rick

So after blowing the college opportunity, I needed yet another new start. Thankfully there is always a restaurant willing to take a chance on you. I had a friend who was working at a Domino's Pizza that was just opening. They needed drivers and manager trainees. It was the best of both worlds. I had a higher pay rate as a manager and I still got to drive and deliver pizzas, too. My buddy, Joe, and I were doing a great job. Our store manager gave the Assistant Manager spot to this girl because he thought she might like him for it. What a joke! She was half as good as we were. Joe got the Day Manager position. I still helped make pizzas during rushes and waited for my chance. She was gone in about two months to a different store and Joe got Assistant Manager and I got Day Manager. We were good, we started kicking butt on food costs and ran a tight ship. Jeff was okay, but he thrived with us in charge. One month he got a $1500 profit sharing bonus, not bad for 1985. We started partying a lot and we had it all. Good pay, long work hours, new cars and a quick trip to the top. That can be a recipe for disaster when pride gets involved. Pride will kick your ass!

We used to sneak in the walk-in and get high. I had a condo, a new truck and life was good. No wisdom or financial savvy yet, but I was paying my bills. I moved out when I was eighteen and I promised myself I would never live with Mom again. I stayed once for about ten days and I was into the condo, never again to dwell under her roof. She was still a lunatic in so many ways. She had let my cool cat Barracuda out once and he never came back. It was heart breaking. I loved that cat. I would have brought him with me but he was gone. So to replace him, she got a rabbit. Rather than putting it in a cage she let it roam the house like a cat. I guess she didn't know, but they have really strong claws for digging up dirt. It didn't take long until this rabbit had shredded the carpet in several places. That was my Mom. We were parting on good terms, but I could not wait to go. It felt like a step backward and I had enough of those lately. Ironically it wasn't long until she bought a house.

She had been saving forever and for the first time since I was seven, she owned property. It was pretty. A no maintenance townhouse with a garage and three levels. It was in a really nice neighborhood. I was proud of her, she was becoming an adult and making good choices. After renting for twenty years, she was making her way prosperous.

Back to Domino's. One night Joe and I were both closing and we had just bought some great pot and we were ready to go party. We had finished the closing chores and all the drivers had left. It was a Wednesday night I think. We were looking at the baggie while in the store and heard a voice. It was Jeff, we were busted! Another one bites the dust. We thought it was over, Jeff just walked out saying, "Oh my God," over and over. We locked up and left. We thought we lost our jobs, so we went for a party time no one would ever forget. Our pride got busy and we jacked it all up. I was scheduled to open the next morning. Jeff didn't fire us on the spot, so I assumed I was supposed to be there. I had really partied hard and was struggling to wake up. I flew out the door and got there a half hour late. I got the store opened on time, but the owner showed up a few hours later and fired me. Joe had a similar situation happen to him. Jeff cut off his own nose and got fired two months later himself. I had done a ton of extra work on my own time to try to build the business, met with different companies, trying to build our lunch business up so I could justify a higher salary. I had made them all a lot of money, but what I did wrong. It was too much. I took responsibility for my actions, but I wasn't happy. I saw how it could go, work hard, save and get your own store. If you ran it well, you had income for a lifetime, maybe financial freedom. Money meant a lot to me, not because of the desire for things, but it represents freedom to me. I saved a lot of my money during high school when I worked 20-30 hours a week at the restaurants, so when the time came, I could go and stay free. I was doing well, then I lost my job and that all changed.

It seemed like every good opportunity was leading to somewhere and then it was taken away. Had I done something wrong to ruin it? Someone had. I noticed this dynamic and I wondered and thought about it a lot. I had no job, so that was easy. I had to give back my new truck to the bank. I remember driving it up there one day, even before the payment was late and telling them, "Here you go, I lost my job, I can't pay for this anymore." I think they were shocked at my honesty. I didn't want something I couldn't afford. It was up to me to do the right thing, even if no one else was. They sold it at auction and paid off my loan. I was free of the burden. I still hate car loans to this day. I prefer to save up for it, not get a loan. I don't like to be in debt to anyone if I can help it. I did layaway once for a winter coat. It was really weird, but I got the one I wanted. It only took six easy payments. Winter wasn't even over yet.

Chapter 19 - Becoming a Man
Marcus

I've always liked women. Let's just get that out there. They're soft in all the right places, they smell good and most of the time they're really nice. I was raised by one and have lived with several. My family is full of strong women, so naturally I gravitate to them. I never abused women like Herb did, but I definitely mistreated them at various times. Herb was trying to get any woman he could at any time. He was always trolling for the next chick and disrespecting my Mom in the process. I always wondered why she put up with it.

One of the early episodes of Star Trek: The Next Generation had a quote in it regarding men's attitudes of women. "Women are highly pleasant things, but after all unnecessary." This attitude has gone on for way too long! Most men do it at some level, regardless of color. Why is it okay to treat women that way? More importantly, why is it okay for men to behave this way? Have we totally abdicated our role to raise and nurture kids and respect women? We as a culture are not calling men up into the people they are. In the Jewish culture, they see young men as a treasure. They spend time with them, they recognize their strengths, their personality and they pour into them in those areas of talent. They get them apprenticeships and help them plan their futures. When they have their bar mitzvah at thirteen or so, they are already men in their culture. Here we just let them play video games until we kick them out of the house at 22 or 27 or 33 or 40...... What the hell is wrong with us? Are we so out of touch, so uncaring towards our men that we do nothing to help them prepare? We've got to start teaching men how to be men or we are finished! When I would go to the bars, something would happen and my alter ego, Big Hank, would show up and I would drink and fight and chase women. Not to love them and be kind to them, usually to get in their pants and see what goodies were inside. I remember the late night booty calls, the friends with benefits scenarios, it was all so easy. After AIDS came, people got a little more cautious but still acted wild. After

Magic Johnson came out as having the AIDS virus, people got a lot more cautious.

My Mom was an enabler, she would help me pay my rent if I was clowning or in between jobs. I seemed to change jobs a lot. She spoiled me. I thought I was a man, but I was acting like a little boy. I needed a good example. Was she feeling guilty? I used it to my advantage every chance I got. I had started hanging out with other guys and ecstasy was getting big then. We were partying and I even got into cocaine a little bit. I let an old friend live with me since he had helped me out a lot in my childhood. Little did I know he was running from a DUI in Virginia Beach. So we started bar hopping and doing the bad kid thing, all the fun with none of the responsibility. I was in Denver to stay and I worked at Dependable Cleaners as a store manager. I went to a Rage Against the Machine concert and there was one song that really spoke to me about the tyranny of this world. I took a copy of the lyrics and faxed it to all the other stores in town. I was fired the same day. Big Hank was starting to make his presence known more and more all the time. I was fighting more. Drinking was big. Petty crimes, too.

Then I went to Starbucks and started selling coffee beans to preppy people. I was the best bean seller they had. I didn't like coffee but it worked. It was close to the University of Denver and that is hot chick central! Next I was a property manager for an apartment complex next to the new Coors Field for the Colorado Rockies baseball team. The whole area was going through a remarkable make over. It used to be skid row, with winos, run down hotels, bombed out buildings, empty warehouses and addicts everywhere. It was really fun to be where things were changing for the better. I met this ballerina there, she was dancing big shows like The Nutcracker. On a date with her, I felt unworthy and nervous. When I'm not Big Hank, I'm shy. It made me feel weirder than usual. I was hanging out with a lot of rich people and still had my lack of confidence issues to overcome. Then I met a beautiful girl from Iowa and we dated some and then her brothers said, "You can't date our sister." "What do you mean I can't date your sister?" I said, "She's a grown woman." She stopped dating me to protect me from them.

It was just another reminder that light skinned or not, there were still a lot of thugs out there wanting to beat me down. Waiting to hate on me. Racism is a curse. How do we get to the point where we are not judged by the color of our skin, but by the content of our character? We have not yet risen up into all that Dr. King and others won for us. We still accept our place as second-class citizens. Why is that? Does anyone know? Why do we act it out and play the fool, filling the prisons with fine young men, having sex with anybody, believing the lies? Brothers and sisters, can we wake up please!

Chapter 20 - USS Missouri
Rick

So after another epic failure with Domino's, I went to the Navy recruiter. I tested out at the highest possible level so I could choose any career path I wanted. I signed up to be a nuclear technician. They are the guys who work on the portable nuclear reactors on the submarines. I was excited, here was a great path to follow. I would learn the science and do my four years, then I could go into private industry and make the $150,000 a year I was expecting to make after the Colorado School of Mines. I couldn't wait to get in. I went to work at a Burger King I had worked in in high school and waited for my day to come. When I got called in for a medical screening, I thought it was just routine, no big deal. So I thought. The fractured ankle I had suffered five years before had returned with a vengeful visit. The doctor disqualified me medically. I couldn't believe it. The same old story all over again. What a letdown! I wanted to travel the world, make my fortune, come of age and grow up! I knew the Navy would help me with those things. I quit my job the next day and then found a Dairy Queen. I really enjoyed the atmosphere and this new thing called a Blizzard. We spent every day bringing smiles to others and putting out the best food in the mall. There wasn't much competition, but I wanted to be the best. It was easy and soon I did all the ordering, scheduling, and managing. I'm rising from the ashes again.

I met this girl Karen at the bar with a group of friends one night. We didn't really talk about it, I just went home with her and stayed for a while. It was weird in a lot of ways, she was six years older and I was kind of immature anyway. She was kind of like a Mom sometimes, but we got along really well. It was nice to have a friend and a lover who understood my world. She had her own issues, but she was nice to me and she was good in bed. I stayed for several months. Yet something wasn't right with us and I knew it. I decided to go visit my dad and try again to connect with him in a way we hadn't before. So I left for Ontario, California. She thought I was going for a visit, but I was going

115

to stay. After a week or two, Dad and I got back into our old habit of throwing shit at each other and he asked me to leave.

Karen was mad when I told her later. I wasn't trying to lie, I just didn't need more drama before going to see my Dad. I grabbed a few clothes and left my suitcases behind. I didn't have anywhere to go, so I went to the park. It was decent there and I wasn't going to freeze to death. I wasn't going to grovel before him and he didn't want me around anyway. So be it. I hated him more and more. The fight came when I was using the phone to call about a job. It had a small long distance charge for the call and he acted like I stole the crown jewels of England or something. It was ridiculous. I called him an asshole. He said, "Get out of my house." So I did, over 75 cents.

I spent most of the day in the park. Dr. Wayne Dyer's books made some sense as I read. Once in a while I would go to the store and buy a little food. I remember a little girl at the store came up to me, (maybe five years old) and asked me, "Where do you live?" "I live in the park," I said. "Why?" she asked. I answered, "Because it's nice there." She looked at me skeptically because she was not convinced. She walked away with her Mom and she looked back at me. I always wondered if she later became a great crusader for the homeless or the downtrodden. She had a passion ignited in her in that moment. It may have defined her destiny, even at five years old.

I went back to the Navy recruiter to try to enlist again. I got all the way to San Diego for boot camp before they discovered my previous attempt. They automatically disqualified me medically. I did get to see the USS George Washington at the dock though. It was so massive, I loved it.

After that I went to live with one of my cousins in Laguna Hills. She had gotten kicked out of her parent's house and there was a family who was taking in strays and troubled kids. Perfect! The Lytle's were really nice and even got me a job fabricating stainless steel into hot dog carts. It was pretty easy work and I didn't have to deal with my Dad. He got me an interview with his boss at General Dynamics. I showed up late on purpose so he would look like the jerk he was. I was only hurting myself.

Life wasn't perfect in Laguna, but I got to see how the rich kids lived. Some of the LA Dodgers and LA Lakers lived in the neighborhood, too. That was a big step up from three people in a one bedroom apartment scenarios that I had lived out with Mom and my sister so many times before. These families had big bucks and no one seemed to want for anything, except purity. Everybody was screwing everybody. I went to my cousin's high school graduation and had no chance with the girls. I wasn't the rich guy and they saw that. Most were cruel in their prejudice. So much privilege and so little commitment to being a quality person to manage it well. Another example of how little we value our children and are not committed to their success. I remember going out to party with her friends a few times and we would do emergency brake slides in the coastal hills. It was fun, but the sheer boredom of having everything they wanted was messing with them. So much for white privilege. I saw that they were lonely kids just like me, the difference was that their money, sex and drugs hid their pain better. I tried it, too, to hide my pain. It didn't work. They just ran wild with privilege and immaturity. The parents were busy and the kids were unsupervised. They had to work for nothing and it was a farce to see them driving around $40,000 cars at seventeen or eighteen years old. Maybe I was just jealous.

So, once again, I saw no meaningful prospects in the land of fruits and nuts (California), so I called Karen. I was tired of being a vagabond and asked if she would send me a plane ticket to Colorado; she did. I said goodbye to my Dad for the last time. I was sick of not being able to connect to him. All he did was drink beer and smoke cigarettes when I was around him. Oh, and feed his precious fish in the pretty pond. He had a house like no other. This was the second one he had built up. It was a bigger show place, in magazines and newspapers, too. He loved to entertain (code word for party) in this backyard paradise. He had a performance area especially for the Hawaiian dancers that came to his yearly luau. He and his second wife Kay hosted it every summer. There were 70,000 gallons of water in his pond. It was so massive he had to put in an island because no filter system existed to process all the water in there. It was a masterpiece. It's too bad some of that time and effort wasn't spent on his son. He had a step son and a step daughter, so he didn't need me anymore. It was a sad reality and I pondered it as I sat by the fish pond and watched his fish. I thought, he loves those fish more than me. I went home and never wanted to see my Dad again, I hated him for never caring about me. I was totally abandoned and full of hate. He never said he was sorry, never made an effort to see who I was. I didn't matter to him. I never did. Please don't do that to your kids, it's a curse and they will hate you for it. Someday you will hate yourself, too.

I came back to Colorado to try again with Karen. Her mom was thinking of getting married and becoming an over the road truck driver with her new husband. There was a 300 acre family farm that needed care taking. Karen's dad had passed away years before and she was the only child. We moved back in together right away. She was pretty savvy and street wise in many ways. She had a four year old daughter and she moved in with us, too. Jessica was a sweet little girl. I really cared about her, I remember what the stepfather of the month club was like, so I wanted it to be something else, something better for her. She was living my sister's life. I had to be different. A different father, a different man. Karen decided to go to Missouri and I went, too. I liked her company, and I was always up for a new adventure anyway. Little did I know what was in store for me.

I had never lived in a small town before. People can treat you a little differently. In my case, a lot differently. In the first few hours we got to work on fixing a rotted out floor. A sign of things to come. It was January and we had to heat the house with a wood stove and use well water. It was quaint and a culture shock for me. Her mom moved up to Iowa leaving us alone in the house. It was 300 acres, and the neighbor farmed the land. There was very little maintenance. The first week I was there, I got in a car wreck. The vehicle I was borrowing slid on the dirt road and hit the other neighbor on the side of his car. I made $25 a month payments on that for a long time. Also Karen got pregnant. It was unexpected to her, but I already knew. I had prayed for her to get pregnant on the way out there. It was the overnight at the motel on the way to Missouri, somewhere in Kansas. I have no idea why I prayed, but I did. I didn't know God, I didn't want a child and Karen and I were early on in our relationship. What was I thinking? I didn't know anything about God. I went to church with my Grandma in the summer a couple times, but that was mostly to eat home baked sweets from the church ladies afterwards.

We started making plans, but our first reaction was to talk about having an abortion. My mind was spinning. I was a mess. Life went on okay, we both had part time jobs and most of our room and board was free. We started having a few struggles and she started working with the I.R.S. in Kansas City, 70 miles away. I changed jobs to a different restaurant and Jessica went to live with her Grandma for a while. It was getting tense. No violence, just drama. She decided to go to Kansas City and have an abortion without telling me. In all fairness, we did discuss it, but she just went and killed my son. His name was David, I knew it in my heart. He wasn't close to being born yet, now he was gone and there was nothing I could do but die inside. It was the worst news ever. I felt like someone punched me in the stomach with an African elephant. I had a staggering sense of loss. I couldn't breathe. I couldn't think. I would cry, I would rage, I was nuts.

If you're thinking about having an abortion, please don't do it. It will be the single worst regret of your entire life, I promise you. It still burns a hole in my soul 25 years later. I cannot shake what was lost. Yes, I forgave her over time and I even forgave myself, but there's someone I never got to meet. My own flesh and blood, lost forever. It's a knife in my heart to this day.

She moved into town and I stayed in the farmhouse. It was a cold and lonely place, spring was in the air, but who cared? All I wanted to do was climb into a bottle of Jack Daniels and drown my sorrows. I changed jobs again and this time, I found all the freaks in town. Everybody treated me like one anyway, so now it was official. Oh yes, if you move into a small town in your 20's and nobody knows you, soon they will. In my experience they will attach all the good or bad of the person that you're with to that evaluation and even make up a few more. It's a strange little sub-culture and I didn't know any better. It can eat you up. It did for me in small town Missouri.

Karen and I split and everyone seemed to have an opinion about her. There was another girl that I liked, but she was married. The only trouble was she didn't act married all the time. She was cute and she would be very flirty, then she would talk about her husband. The mixed signals drove me bonkers. She worked at one of the restaurants with me. Another time, this restaurant had a party at someone's house. There was a keg of beer and about 20 of us. The weird thing was that after a while everybody sat down and watched porn together. It was not foreplay to an orgy or anyone touching each other. It was just like watching any other movie, except it wasn't. I think it was one of the stranger experiences in my life. I looked at the two cute girls and they were watching it closely, but no one was doing anything. No one was saying anything. No one was breathing. After a little while I left and never again partied with those people. It was peculiar. Even for my world. It was just plain weird.

The summer there was long and hot. I remember one day working in the kitchen in July and losing about fifteen pounds from sweating so much. I was working two jobs now, just drowning my angst in work and booze, anything to forget David's loss and the fullness of my failure. I hated to see Karen by this point. She was in town getting ready to shack up with some dude. I hated my life and once again it was proving to be a letdown. I was so sick of it, I started looking for a way out. Any way out. I didn't think anything good could happen anymore. Losing my son had been profound and ugly. Our shame is our poison that we drink, day after day and we wonder why we're sick and faulty and troubled all the time. We are causing our own downfall because we refuse to do the right things. Summer was winding down and I was starting to get homesick. I had to make a plan to get out of here. Anything was better than stalling around and drinking every night, but how? I didn't have any money saved. What a stupid year in a stupid life. What was I here for anyway?

Chapter 21 – Aspen
Marcus

After some self-destructive challenges in Denver I quit Starbucks and went to work for Gensler, a big architectural firm. I did accounting. Spreadsheets and ergonomic chairs, it was a good gig with travel and benefits. I would move up to Aspen two years later. That was a party town on steroids. Me and a buddy fit right in from day one. I started working part-time as a bouncer at this club at night. I fell hopelessly in love with the Aspen nightlife. I met so many cool people there and reunited with many old high school friends. I met Reggie Jackson, one of my heroes and Michael Jordan, Mariah Carey, Goldie Hawn, Kate Hudson, Catherine Zeta-Jones, Jack Nicholson and hundreds more stars. I soon became the head bouncer at this club. I got lots of attention from the beautiful ladies. Bouncing was great, everybody was rich and famous. There was really no competition or drama like other clubs. It was pretty chill. Then I got into trouble, my first real trouble. It was called felony fraud because I was writing checks that were fraudulent, adding hours for my friends at a fitness club. Off to the Aspen County Jail! Then I found another club where drinking and the cocaine were flowing like water. After a bit, we were selling drugs right out the door of the club. Big money coming in every night, I thought I was the King Matador. I started doing some coke to help me stay up and was drinking all night, too. We would go over to rich people's houses and do cocaine with them. Everyone was so cordial. There would be a big bowl with cocaine in it, just go help yourself like it was chips and salsa! So very crazy! Sometimes I got very little sleep, and the profits started going up my nose. I stayed up more and more. Sleep is essential I discovered. I would not normally hang out with these people, but cocaine was the great equalizer. I was making judgement errors, having regrets. One time we were too loud and the cops came, I had an 8 ball of cocaine and I was scared. I handed it off to my friend right under the cop's nose. I knew I had a warrant for a fight and the coke would send me straight to jail long term! Somehow he missed the hand off and I was free. I got so lucky, someone was looking out for me.

At this point my sister, Zhalih, was very sick. She was in a hospital in Pittsburgh and Mom tracked me down to let me know she was going to pass away. I tried to get to Denver to get on a flight to Pittsburgh. I hadn't talked to my family in a long time and part of me didn't want to deal with it, but she was my sister and I loved her. We tried getting down the mountain fast. I had a friend whose dad was retired from United Airways and he had a buddy pass for the flight and he had a Ferrari so we blasted off down the hill. On the way, the Ferrari lost a fuel line and we coasted into the gas station in Copper Mountain. I was afraid I had missed my chance to say goodbye. Just then somebody else pulled into the gas station and said they were going to the airport in Denver. What an amazing turn of events! I rode with them down there and got on the next flight. I got to sit in first class and live it up with free drinks all the way there. I got to the hospital and a pastor was praying over her, Holy Spirit moved and miraculously, my sister didn't die. She got ambulatory again, but still was very sick.

She was awake three days later and I came in and we talked. We talked about our childhood and she told me how she had come to accept Jesus Christ. She said Jesus had given her the strength to move past all the garbage we went through. She asked me why I did all the things I did. I had no answer. I think she knew she was dying and was looking for a way to help me find the peace that she had found. She went to rehab for a while and made some progress. I had three cousins who were also selling cocaine at the time. Aspen was becoming St. Louis revisited. Isn't that a stupid way for us to define ourselves. Basing our value on how risky and reckless our behavior can be. Like that makes us tough or heroic or something. Why did I ever think that was a good thing? Why do we continue to live it out every day, year after year? I think we need to act differently now. We are better than this, but we're not acting like it. This mindset of crime and sorrow has to end. That's why black lives matter, not just because we are being discriminated against, but because we are doing the right things. There is a big difference. We matter, but let's stop focusing on every negative. Let's stop choosing destruction.

Yes some people will abuse us, but if we're doing the right things, it's going to make them look like the losers they are for treating us poorly. It's the heart of what Dr. King was saying. Judge us for how we behave, not for the color of our skin alone. Maybe we forget that. Maybe we never learned it. It is time. If we're robbing a liquor store and a cop shoots us, it's our fault. If we're coaching a kid's sports team and we got shot, then be outraged and demonstrate, burn the flag or whatever. See the difference? Do something good.

Some of our descendants were slaves, yes it's true. They suffered horribly for no good reason and we still do in some ways today. The Jews have been persecuted for centuries because of their religion. Not for something they did wrong. The Native Americans were killed, robbed, threatened and relocated simply because they were in the way. They were slaughtered for having land and not for anything they did wrong. Poor people, ex-offenders, a lot of people struggle. Do you see my point? We're not the only ones. We only act like we are. Poor us, everybody messed up my life. Stop it! My God people, can we please freaking grow up? We are more than that, better than that. Everybody has been treated like crap at some point. We all have. This negative mindset is going to kill us all off. What if we focus on the good instead? What if we keep our families together, go to college, help our communities, save for the future and make a difference. If we keep living like players and going to the club, being immoral and forgetting to make our kids our main focus, we're never going to improve our place in this world. If we go that way, then it's our fault, not the slave owners.

Do you know that several million immigrants came to America a hundred years ago from Europe and other places? From 1904 to 1914, over twelve million people flooded into the US as legal immigrants. Most years averaged 300,000-400,000 new immigrant residents every year. 1991 was the highest year ever with over 1,800,000 coming to America according to migrationpolicy.org. These are the legal residents. They did citizenship the way you're supposed to. Now in America, we have border jumpers. We want you to be here, just do it the right way. Europeans came here in force to escape and to search for opportunities. They have made America what it is today, and they did it legally. When

123

others come here we want them to come the right way, too. We blacks, we're already here. Some of our families have been here for over 200 years! Sometimes we act like we just got here off the slave boat. We're not slaves anymore! Say it with me, we're not slaves anymore! President Lincoln signed a law that outlawed that in 1863 with the Emancipation Proclamation. Why do we still live, act and expect life as though we are slaves? Let the days of apathy, negativity, sorrow, regret and shame be over forever. We are not slaves! We're not sex slaves, work slaves, we're not slaves to the world or any group. We're not slaves to a system or an ideology, we are free! Adopting a victim mindset and looking only at the circumstances is never going to grow us up into a people to be revered and emulated. It's going to keep the chains on. I for one am sick of it. I will not be a victim anymore. Not from Herb, or my Mom or my birth Dad or the neighborhood, the white people, the black people or the government, the culture, or even myself, no more! Speak this out with me if you want to be free, too!

Identity Proclamation For Emancipation!
We're free! Say it! Walk in it! Believe it! Live it! Brothers and sisters, we're free!
We are equal and free! A gift to the world!
We will not be manipulated by fear, hate or regret any longer!
We are full of life, hope and peace is ours!
We are perfectly made, amazingly powerful and wonderful!
We are intelligent, wise, special and knowledgeable!
We have what it takes already inside us to be amazing!
We are able to learn, to grow and to thrive!
We will always succeed when we love ourselves and others!
We have overcome and we will overcome!
We will not be defined by how others act or treat us!
We will do our part and we will do what is right!
We matter because we are human, not because of our skin color!
We will rise and fall on our ability to love our children, ourselves and others!

We give thanks to those who went before and those who will come after us!
Our words and actions will be life affirming, always becoming and filled with kindness!
Let us be searched and known that we are people of integrity and goodness!
Now! My heart and mind are open to receive all the greatness of who I am!
I believe in good things happening all around me from now on!
I believe that living the right way will benefit me and the whole world!
I will bring light into this world and chase away the darkness!
God is for us, He brought us this far and He can take us all the way!
We break off these generational curses over us!
We separate from the past and from all that was done to us and our families!
We call forth a new future of freedom, blessing and honor for ourselves and our people!
We walk in healing, wholeness and new life from this day forward!

Your words have power to change your destiny! If we don't say it and believe it others won't either! Believe it! Say it! Live it! Change your world by the words you say, what you believe and the actions you do. Then you can be free and stay free. Let's do it! Remember you don't attract what you want, you attract what you are! You are loved and you are special, live every day like you believe it! Act it out and then attract what you are. Say this statement every day, several times a day, until it starts to change you for the better. You can become new, but you have to believe it and repeat it! A new you is near, waiting to arrive and take hold forever. It's a powerful season of change for the better. Let's activate it. A whole new future awaits us!

Chapter 22 – Chocolate
Marcus

In Aspen I could do just about anything I wanted. I continued the process of medicating my pain away, not dealing with it. Herb had been found guilty of sexually abusing my sister Zhalih and he went to prison in Virginia. Finally something in my life made sense. Where were the police and social workers way back when? I wonder why they didn't defend us, free us, kill us, at least do something.

It seems there's always a fine line between hero and psychopath. Do you need some of each to succeed in this life? Everyone in my family is like that. One cousin has done well, but he's the biggest womanizer there is. His father did the same thing and beat his mom, too. She is a sweet lady. It's just a freak show. Is that your family, too? I'm sick of it. Most of the families run around, and nobody's home with these kids. They're all just running wild with girlfriends on the side when they're married. Nobody cares to do what's right. It's a free-for-all. I don't know how to change the minds of millions of people in America except to tell them the truth. Got any ideas?

About four months after my sister was in Pittsburgh, she got sick again and passed away. I was able to be there for her at the end. Her death rocked me to my core. It still does today. I felt incredible guilt for being away, for not defending her, for not killing Herb to keep her safe. I didn't want to see my family anymore, it was too emotional, too painful, I was too angry. Like a Daisy Cutter bomb going off in me every time I saw them. Her funeral was the worst. It was row after row of somber people, most of whom I didn't want to be around. I would have been happy to walk out of that room and never see them again.

After my sister died, I moved out of Aspen and got to the end of something. The cocaine was too much. I needed to change or I would really hurt myself. My conversations with Zhalih impacted me when she spoke to my heart like no one else could. In Glenwood Springs there was an ad for a job at the hospital. The scene was different there. People smoked a lot of weed, but it was calmer somehow. There was a penthouse apartment and I lived there. It was a good location for life in a new way. They did a urine analysis to qualify for the job and I had been away from cocaine long enough to be clear and finished my probation. Losing my sister had started motivating me to clean up my act. Mom was dating some new guy and he was verbally abusive. Mom finally decided maybe Herb was wrong. She mourned the loss of her daughter and we talked about the past. She was learning the price that we all paid.

My new position at the hospital was working in the O.R. cleaning instruments. It was easy and different. We cleaned surgical machines as well. It was still a party, but nothing even close to Aspen. I began to breathe a little. It was better than sitting on the couch depressed all the time. It also felt good to do something that helped people again. I was tired of always serving myself. I worked hard. Then I got an offer I never expected. Valley View hospital had a radiology program. They liked me and they offered to send me to school. I jumped at the chance. I became class president and I got a scholarship. I even won a national award. I worked hard and graduated near the top of my class. Suddenly people wanted me, I was a hot commodity. I went to a national conference in Dallas to receive the award. I had doors open anywhere I wanted to go, but I decided to stay near Denver. I interned at three places, but I never studied for final certification or tool test. Old life showed up again and I started booking bands with my friend Slick, the Emperor and his band ESP. Goodbye new life.

We started hanging out in Lakewood, Colorado. They had a late night bar scene on Colfax Avenue there. I met this guy who showed me how easy it was to cook up and sell crack. I was developing my Apple computer business skills by taking classes at the stores and then we began stealing programs, computers, hard drives and iPods. My friends and I would take them to the resellers and get top dollar since they were brand new. I would make about $3000 a day. Who doesn't want to be the man? It was my family tradition taking center stage. Many days I would drive to Fort Morgan and I had a trunk full of stolen goods and zips of methamphetamines. One time being pulled over and I would have gone away forever. I didn't care, I was reckless! iPods were brand new then and I got good at stealing since they had no alarms or security then. I would trade gangsters, drug lords and coke dealers Apple computers for cocaine. I would cook it up and sell it. I would smoke it or give it away to increase my customer base. My three cousins were still testing my blackness, since they thought I was a white boy. I had to prove to them and to myself that I could do it. That I was black enough to do it. I was messed up enough in my head to have to prove it to them again and again. What was wrong with me? I was so hurt and reckless. I had a bodyguard with a gun and an emerald green Audi A4 with heated seats. I would go from drug spot to drug spot checking my accounts.

I was a professional criminal well into my thirties and I was still mad at my Dad. I was partying with strippers, night people and prostitutes in my house. They were stealing checkbooks and my roommate's personal items. I was still expecting them to be like normal people. I was so naive and this was not Aspen. They tried to steal my stuff, too, and use me. I cruised the tough spots, selling drugs and doing drugs especially down at the triangle. Colfax Avenue was the worst scourge in Denver – fifty miles of drugs, prostitutes, alcohol, everything wrong with the world and hearts like mine.

I was in rebellion from everything. My friend had a niece named Wendy and I confided in her. She was very nice to me and helped me a lot after my sister's death. We moved in together when I went to radiology school. We got baptized together. She wanted us to get married. She knew I was doing wrong and she wanted me to get out of it. I became her quest. I told her I didn't want to be married again, but she didn't listen. She liked telling everybody we were engaged and trying to save me from the rogues of Lakewood. She pleaded with me to go back and finish school. I had just a few things to complete my school, but making money and doing drugs had a strong pull on my wounded spirit. I loved the economic difference in my life. I wasn't interested in making $13 an hour. It's retarded to start your criminal career in your thirties but that was me. It's hard to justify $100 a day when you're making $3000 doing crime. I see why people do it because I did it. The heart has to deal with the pain or the behavior will follow into many dangerous and difficult places.

I just wasn't feeling my emotions that much anymore. Wendy picked me and a guy I barely knew up at Cherry Creek Shopping Center. This guy told her we can pay him $500 for a pound of cocaine and that's ridiculously cheap. I wasn't buying it, but Wendy said, "I have the money for it." What was she thinking?! Normally I wasn't going to do business unless I knew someone pretty well. So this guy gets the cocaine and brings it out to the car. I got so sick. Then I noticed a cop car down the street. So we dropped him off at the Denver West Motel on West Colfax Avenue. Wendy was driving, and she took all the cocaine from my pocket. They searched me up and down. It felt like a set up and it was. It turned out this was a trap house. They busted you and used that as leverage so you turned in the next guy up the ladder of drug dealers. They said, "You're going down." If I confessed that it was mine, I was looking at serious hard time. I had a decent rap sheet so maybe twenty years. She volunteered the money to buy it. I didn't even want to go, but for some reason I did. I still feel guilty about what happened. It was her money and I figured they would go easy on her because she didn't even have a parking ticket and she was a Dartmouth graduate. It was a total set up from the get go. I saw up close how the drug thing worked and the price you paid. It was destroying me and now destroying others, too.

I was distraught. For somebody to get in trouble who had never been in trouble before was awful. I hated that she got mixed up in trouble and I was out of control again. I was in deep shit with the DA. He said, "If you want to get her out of trouble then I want you to tell me who your drug dealer is." I didn't talk. They wanted me to wear a wire, but I wouldn't. So they threatened me with prison. Every day I was making money selling drugs nonstop to forget. I knew I had to change my life again. I was still selling stolen goods, the cops were on to me and the end was near. Wendy took the rap for the cocaine.

I was baptized into Jesus a year earlier with Wendy, but I never read the Bible. It would have helped me learn and grow. I would hear these voices. Maybe it was God. I would get scared. God was talking, but I wasn't listening. After two days of no sleep, I was dropping off drugs on my regular route. I met this girl and she persuaded me to run up to Westminster to pick up some money she was owed, then on to Erie,

Colorado with a dealer named Chocolate I had met the day before. I was swerving in the car, so I got pulled over by the Erie police. There was a lot of new construction out there in 2006. A rain storm was coming in quickly. Who the hell was I? What a joke I had become! Drugs were in the car and it was Friday. I decided to run for it and I drove over this cop's foot trying to get away. I drove around in a circle with the weird construction. The rain was pounding. I was looking for a way out, any way out. I was desperate, lost and now hunted.

Chapter 23 - The Hole
Marcus

It was a high speed car chase. I was trapped and my heart was pounding. I leapt from the car and hid behind a garage in someone's backyard. Running from Herb had taught me how to hide. The cops caught Chocolate and then brought out a helicopter to search for me. I could hear them talking. The guy who owned the garage came out and tried to grab me and I ran through a green belt. I never saw his face. I ran through a muddy field and then it started pounding rain again. I slipped into this deep hole. The dirt was wet and I fought to get out. The more I struggled, the worse it got. I went back down into the mud and it sucked me even deeper. I couldn't breathe. I got pulled in, down to my knees. It was like quicksand. I felt like I was drowning in mud. It felt like forever. Maybe an hour or two. Fighting the mud, the same way I used to fight Herb and everything else. I'm like, "God I need your help, you know."

All of a sudden I was being pulled up out of the mud. I don't know how, but it was God. I was thinking, "I'm gonna be real quiet and crouch down." I don't want to minimize this part because I was there for an hour or more. My mind was racing and I was hyperventilating. Here I was, surviving a high-speed car chase just waiting for the worst to happen. I was freaking out, cracking up and starving. I was doing drugs non-stop. I was in renal kidney failure and I didn't even know it. I was close to dying in the mud. The police finally caught me. My crime spree was over. I got charged with five felonies and I was 35 years old. I couldn't get out of this one, or overcome myself anymore. I had been burying my stuff, medicating my pain for a long time and now it was judgement day. Now I was in a position I had never been in before. I was looking at hard time. I had an ocean of unforgiveness in my hardened heart. I had a lot to make up for. I had PTSD before they had a name for it. I had to call my Mom and tell her my news. What was chasing me here? All this stuff was going on and I had to ask myself, "Why are you dealing drugs? Why do you have all this stolen merchandise? What are you doing Marcus?" All the times Herb said I was stupid and I would never do anything good, manifested. I believed the lies he told me and now prison was looming.

Knowing the truth is important to keep yourself free. When you tell someone they are stupid, they will be. If you tell yourself you're no good, you will be no good. It may take a while to appear, but it will, sometimes with a vengeance. Speak encouragement to others. Don't believe the lies, believe that you are good. God doesn't make junk! He makes beautiful, wonderful children who struggle at times, but He loves us! He really loves us! He will help us get back on track no matter what we've done. When I stopped running, I had a chance to reflect. I finally reached the end of myself. Here I had graduated college and everything I ever wanted was right in front of me. Instead I was arrested again.

I ended up going to the hospital to treat my kidneys. It was a brand new hospital in Lafayette and I thought I could leave anytime I wanted to. I was in police custody in the hospital and receiving kidney treatments. Mama called back. She heard my phone message of what happened and she was in tears. She told me I had to stop this behavior and she was right. I made up my mind that day. I promised myself I would stop this madness. Yet here I was trying to escape hospital custody by taking car keys out of a doctor's office. I went to the parking area, but I couldn't find the car. I just needed to stop running. No matter where I thought I was going to go it didn't matter, because they would find me. The police would chase me down. My mind was set on escaping and if I had, in a couple days I would have died. My kidneys were that bad. Every hour thirteen people die from addiction. That could have been me, too. But again I was spared. The partying and not eating did major damage to my body and I felt horrible. I spent quite a while in the hospital and then I told the Erie Police Officer everything I had done the last six months. He wrote it all down. So when I got done healing, it was time to go to jail and accept my fate. The five felonies I had been charged with were adding up to a potential forty years in the Colorado Department of Corrections. Oh my God, that's the rest of my life, I'm 35, I could be 75 when I got out of prison. I cried and cried. My life was over and it was my fault.

I went to county jail to start serving my lesser charges first. I was nervous and freaked out, but like I promised the Lord, I picked up the Bible. That's when I really got into church services and God's word. I found there's no better service than serving someone coming into jail or prison for the first time. It was modeled for me by others. You never forget those people who help you find your way in prison. I have never forgotten any of them, and I wanted to be that person for others. In the midst of the scariest days of my life, changes started in me. The worst possible scenario was bringing a good result in my heart and mind. Prison was hard, but I was going to have to get used to it. Detoxing off the drugs was challenging, too. Unforgiveness was kicking my ass again. Bitterness, anger, and sorrow were creeping in. What was I going to do? Being incarcerated was hard, but I was going to have to learn a new way to deal with life. It was me and the Lord now. I needed His help and He turned the next eleven months into a long Bible Study for me. I whole new way to look at life, through His eyes.

Chapter 24 – Father
Marcus

In our experience, Black families and German families have this harshness built into them. I guess a lot of subcultures do. The brutality of my stepfather had made me bitter. He would cut me down every chance he got. He was awful and I learned his ways well. My ways needed to change. What finally made the difference for me was learning that I have a real father in heaven who loves me unconditionally. I needed a new way of seeing things, I needed freedom and a totally different experience in my life. I needed God. I needed a real loving father not a lunatic. I became a student and a teacher of the Bible in every facility I went into and talked about the love of God.

I spent eleven months bouncing from county jail to county jail. I stayed in the bible. It should have been the worst time of my life but God keeps showing up and I started trusting Him. I had to, who else is going to help me here? That was a new experience for me. He is not just a figment of my imagination, or a cute story. He's actually a real-life experience! That's the big difference. I love teaching people about the Bible. I like to make it real. It's not just an old story. It's a relationship with pure love. When He shows up, everything is different. I met him at a Bible study in prison. I met him in a mud hole in the rain. I started to realize He was in all kinds of different places in my life. He was with me chained to the trash can. He was with me in the clubs. He was with me marching in the rain, playing football, learning the truth and through all the struggles. He was with me doing cocaine with hookers. He was with me when I ran away. He was with me stealing iPods. He was with me now in prison. He was with me! Then I realized He was always with me.

They played a series of videos in prison called "Experiencing God." I had so many questions to answer. Now my mind was clearing and my body was healing, it was awesome. I always loved learning and now I was a sponge on steroids! Being drug free, My IQ returned and I loved discussing everything and having answers. Not to be smart, but because I really wanted to know, I needed to know. Nothing in my life ever made sense before. It was starting to. I loved being able to help others who had questions, too. There's healing in helping others. I wanted to know the deeper questions of life, and so I asked the leader all about the Trinity, sin, slavery, abuse, crime, guilt, shame, honor and more. I wanted to know every answer to every question. I loved being able to tell people the truth. In the morning when I could be sleeping I was walking around the courtyard. I was learning about confession. I just kept praying for forgiveness for everything I had done to God. Yes it was against Him. I could blame all my choices on Herb, my Mom and a thousand other things; but I had to discover and to confess that most of it was my fault. Yes, most of it was my fault and I had done it to God. He's the one we sin against, not just whoever our victim was. I sinned against God and I needed to find forgiveness from Him.

I prayed about forgiveness for my behaviors, a failed marriage and relationships, lack of reconciliation, my family and my sons. I failed them all. For all the mistakes and poor choices I had made. For all the people I fought and fed drugs to, for all the girls I mistreated and all the lives I ruined. The tally was mounting. It was massive. I learned a new kind of regret and grief. People that I have met along my journey who helped me were amazing. I talked to a chaplain and other inmates about how they changed their lives. I was committed to permanent change. I needed to know how, and they helped me to do it! After coming through the kind of garbage I had, I needed a lot of help to learn a better way to live. I wanted to be just like those guys. I wanted to read the word, I wanted to change my thoughts and my mind. I wanted to change my heart and my emotions. I didn't want to be evil, wounded or faulty anymore.

I wrote my Mom letters and they were basically sermons about how to change your life. It was an important part of my process. There was a correspondence bible study course I devoured with a zeal I didn't know I had. I couldn't get enough Jesus. Mom started telling me I was different. I was determined and I had God now. I didn't want to fail. I had Jesus in my soul and I got to know Him in such an intimate place. We were so close. I was learning God's ways. Other people started coming to Christ, too! At first I thought it was me opening their eyes, but as I got older, I learned it was the Holy Spirit reaching people's heart and minds. I was just a vessel, a boat He sails in, a cup He pours water out of. Like a glove for His hand to fit into.

The whole time I was in jail I pursued Jesus, and then finally it became time to see the judge. I wrote him a long letter because I had eleven months to prepare. I had court cases all over and what they do is combine all the cases and run them concurrently. I was the mastermind of the theft but I wasn't stealing anymore, I was using other people to do it. I minimized it when I saw the judge and it was game on. I put the piece of paper down and spoke to him from my heart. I just told him all the stuff I was going to do when I got out. I told him how it's going to go, about how things are different now. He said, "I could hold you for what you did anyway and we can pin the charges on you at trial." What would he decide? My life was literally in his hands and forty years is a long time. I was scared and unsure of the outcome. I knew that with God, everything would be okay.

Chapter 25 - The Trees
Rick

I vowed to myself I wouldn't spend Christmas in Missouri. It was a place I hated more each day. One day I was burning trash at the old farm and the wind came up unexpectedly. That was rule number one: *don't burn trash when it's windy*. There was some dry grass near the fire pit and pretty soon it caught fire. Putting out a fire with well water was very challenging. The water came out like a trickle and the fire got ahead of me. I tried to contain the lines but the fire kept spreading. The country fire department was at least forty minutes away. The dry tree next to the garage caught on fire. I didn't want the garage to go up, so I worked on that and got it put out. In the meantime the fire kept burning grass and got over to the chicken house, while I'm distracted with the garage. There was plenty of fuel for the fire because chicken poop is a supreme heat source and very flammable.

Just about that time, Michael, the neighbor, came by on his tractor. He was a nice guy who farmed the land. He looked over at me and said in his best drawl, "Whaaaat are youuuuuu doing Rickkkkkk?" I looked at him and said, "I'm burning down the farm Michael." He turned toward me not missing a beat and said, "You're doing a pretty good job of it." He drove the tractor over to the chicken house and pushed it in on itself, and it burned fast now. The flames were seven feet tall! About this time Karen showed up and went into a rant. I said, "Either help or shut up please." We still got along well, in spite of everything that had happened. I just found it hard to look at her. She knew she was wrong, but it was too late to fix it now. My son was dead. My heart was broken

I had gotten used to the failures now, the car wrecks, the rejection, the shit life. One after another they came. I had spent the summer drinking too much and working a ton of hours. Now it was mid October 1987. The trees were changing and the colors were different here. In Missouri they have a lot of reds, browns and maroons. In Colorado there are a lot of yellow and gold colors when the trees change. My car had a part go out, so I started walking to work while it was down.

It was about four miles so I left early to get there on time. This particular day it was sunny and mild. The sunshine felt good on my wounded spirit. The walk was nice, too, it cleared my head from the heavy drinking of Jack Daniels I was doing. Everything there was two lane roads, but there wasn't much traffic. About half way through the walk was a bridge over a small river. When I got there I looked down the river and the tree colors were astonishing. It's like I had never seen color before. The brightness of the hues, the perfection of the light and the pure majesty of that moment stopped me in my tracks. I crossed the bridge and I spoke out loud. "Why do you waste your time? Why do you make these trees so beautiful? We just drive by at fifty-five miles an hour and we never notice, why do you waste your time?" I had never spoken out loud to God before. I'm not sure why I did. I soon discovered something. Once you ask the first question, it's really easy to ask God all the rest. "Why has my life been a mess? What was going on? Why did everything seem to go down the toilet? What am I here for?" I had an endless supply of questions, a lifetime worth saved up and waiting to be out of me. I felt a presence come along side of me. I didn't see or hear anything but the Lord had come near. I needed him more than I ever thought was possible. I talked and talked, all He did was listen. Oh, how He listened! No one had ever done that before, really listened. I had a lot to say and He listened to every word. He will do the same for you.

I went to work and had a regular day, but I felt different. That night I got a ride home, but no partying. I went home to the farmhouse. I sat down in the living room and it was painfully quiet. There was a picture of Jesus on the wall. It was Him walking on the water. The painter had the light coming from behind Him above the waves. It seemed to beckon me. I walked over to where the picture was and looked at it. It had power. I looked down and saw a bible sitting there. I had never read the Bible before. I picked it up and opened it. I read what I saw and it was Matthew 4:4 "man does not live by bread alone, but by every word that proceeds from the mouth of God." I closed the book and asked God, "What does that mean?" He didn't answer, but He was there. I felt His kindness and love all around me. I opened the bible again and not knowing what to do, I started reading the Gospel of Matthew. I read the whole book that night, all 28 chapters. I learned so much in a few hours. Suddenly, my life made sense. I understood that people were evil and had a propensity to do the wrong thing. I discovered that God's ways are much different than ours. Jesus hung out with all the lowlifes. All the losers, misfits and outcasts. He was not ashamed of them, He cared for them. That was me, too. I learned how much people don't care about each other, but He wasn't like that. I liked Him, I needed Him, I wanted to be like Him. I wanted to be with Him! He was so welcoming but he didn't fix my mess in the first few hours. He showed me the way out and encouraged me to run through the open door. I did! With reckless abandon! I was different from the first day!

Unlike most people, I didn't go to church. I didn't watch the religion hawkers on TV. It was just me and Jesus. It was such a sweet time. I began coming to life for the first time. It was a startling difference. I didn't know what freedom was, but I was beginning to learn. I felt like a 7000 pound gorilla had gotten off my back. My circumstances had not changed, but how I saw them did. It wasn't about the abuse, neglect and sorrow anymore. It was about *what do I do now?* I still hated my parents and my life, but now it was up to me. I could stay as the victim or I could become something else. All up to me. I stopped drinking and I decided to go home to Denver. That was a good start.

Try reading the Bible if you never have, it will change your life, too! Jesus didn't ask me to do any religious things, He just loved me. I felt like I could hear His voice all the time. I started telling people about how good it could be. Some misunderstood or told me to go screw myself, but I didn't care. It was real! I had this powerful experience with God and I was remade. I didn't have religion or a set of rules to follow, I had a friend closer than a brother. I had a companion that wanted the best for me and had the skills, tools and patience to help me get there. There was nothing I couldn't do. There is nothing I can't do!

I called my old boss and got my job back at Dairy Queen. He had accused me of stealing money out of the till, but I took a polygraph and passed it a year and a half before, so he hired me on the spot. I had a job, a plan and hope for first time in a long time, maybe ever. I told Karen I was leaving, she volunteered to drive me back and get her stuff that was at my Mom's house. It was awkward silence for much of the drive, but we got there on December 23rd. No Christmas in Missouri, just like I promised myself! The first of many promises to come true. We loaded her stuff and she walked out of my life forever. I hope things worked out well for her. I had to move back in with Mom, but she was busy nursing Jerry through a series of health issues. She left me alone for the most part. I had a job and I did it very well.

I was sharing Jesus with all my old friends. They wanted to party and I was good without it. I still hung out, but I was unique now and they started feeling uncomfortable around me. They never said it out loud, but I could tell, me and Jesus weren't welcome. I guess that's been true for 2000 years. It took a long time for me to realize, but I actually preferred it that way. I'd rather have one real friend then hundreds who are circumstantial. Those people are only friends when it benefits them. I don't need friends like that anymore, I've had enough of being used in my life. Even so, I was a little lonely. I wanted to be someone special so I made friends with the new people at work, the other employees in the mall, anyone I could. I discovered relationships were a great way to go. They really help to build up a new identity. I had dreams coming forth. I was becoming someone new. I was searching for that special treasure, that perfect pearl, that life changing scenario and it was happening.

Chapter 26 – Verdict
Marcus

I was involved, but not doing the actual stealing. All the county District Attorneys talked together and the judge gave me three years of prison time. A total miracle! I was looking at 40 years! I finally went to the prison, after months in county jail and the first week was tough. They sent me to the worst place they could, Sterling Correctional Facility. It was a level five facility. Basically, all the worst offenders in the state were there. Level one is the lowest security level and five is the highest. It was a big change from county jail. These guys were lifetime criminals. I started on the high side at first with the lifers: murderers, assault with a deadly weapon, bank robbers, rapists, domestic violence, all the cream of the crop. There were skinheads and rowdies, gangsters and motorcycle outlaws, white collar criminals and mental patients. There were also a lot of guys like me, beaten, abused, forgotten, neglected, messed up with no dad or a tyrant for a father. There was something familiar in all of it. Sadly familiar.

All we have is a few days here on earth: we sing, we dance, we love, we live and we die. It's a circle of life. My behavior started changing. I started getting looser and looser. Like I was finally getting comfortable in my own skin for the first time. The pod I was in had Bible studies. It was good, but the weird thing is, it didn't feel like real life to me somehow. I had a different feeling than the leader did. We were going back and forth talking about God. Those were some great conversations. The guys were soaking it up like sponges. I'm doing my time with Jesus now, let's talk about it some more!

Sterling houses about 2500 guys. We're having church services there and a group from Denver's Church in the City came to be with us. They were awesome! They really loved people and did a lot of outreach to the homeless and ex-offenders in the inner city. They were a great resource and real friends. That's one of the problems with ministry sometimes, they are trying really hard, but they don't get to know the people and miss the point. Relationships really change lives, not service alone. After a while I got moved to the low side. It was not like the high side, two guys in a 6 x 10 cell, it was more like a dorm house with your own room. You have a roommate but with more space and maybe carpet, too. On the high side you're with guys who are never getting out. What a tough mindset that is. You're here in prison and you're never getting out. That makes a long time to think about the past. I didn't want to live in the past, I wanted to go forward and live my life for the first time. My zeal was contagious. Even to the lifers. Jesus was making me new.

When I was on the low side, I met Craig. I heard about him forever and I finally got to know him. He helped guys get ready to get out and he did aftercare ministry from the inside. I met Joaquin, Karius and Steve. All of us guys were going to church together and ministering to people in the yard. I was playing cards with two Spanish guys. They became obnoxious because they thought I cheated. "Did you call me a cheater? Do you want to fight about it? I got you chump, come on!" I growled. We went to my room and he began the fight. I went straight to the hole. I was at the lowest point in my life. I was full in my shame and regret, acting like the old me when I was representing Jesus. I was so sad and lonely, but the difference was, I had the word of God. Someone passed me their old dirty Bible and I read James. I was in the dark, but there was this little light that came into my cell.

I was in the hole on Thanksgiving Day of 2007 and I wasn't alone anymore. I said to God: "You've got to get me out of here, please!" I was so overwhelmed in shame and I didn't want to fight any more. I didn't want to be that person anymore. Once you fight in prison everybody wants a turn with you, it can ruin your chances for ever getting out. So a knock came to the door a few days later and the guard said, "It's your time to go see the Parole Board, Mr. Weaver!" Are you kidding me? I didn't expect to see sunlight anytime soon. I was asking myself more questions. What are you gonna do with your life Marcus? How are you going to get out of here? I think I'm gonna save the world and do all these things right! I'm being so sweet and helping people all I can but now I'm in the hole. What's up with that? Who was I really? Was life ever going to make sense? Could I be real? Could I be for Jesus all the time?

Prison, basically, is a huge place when you get there and it gets smaller each day. The walls start closing in. You don't talk about getting out. You have to be real careful about sharing your info with people. If people know you might be getting out soon, they might make it more difficult or try to block you from ever leaving, just for spite. There are wisdoms and real rules that are in place inside the walls and you have to learn them fast. There is a hierarchy and ways to do things to keep you safe. There's people to avoid and silence is a good skill to learn quickly. Keep your eyes open and your mouth shut. People are in prison for a reason. Some of them are not nice. It's just a weird place but there's more opportunities for Jesus than anything else. I got into that Jesus group of people. It was nice to belong. The sky was so bright one night before Christmas you could see all the stars in Sterling. We sang "Oh Holy Night" and that is one of my favorite songs. It was peaceful! I loved the word of God and I really loved the work that He gave me to do. We were mentoring others and life really made sense for the first time. People's lives were changing in the worst environment there is. That's the power of God's love! Prison meant freedom for me and others. Isn't God funny? His ways are so different.

Chapter 27 - Honey Bee
Rick

My mom worked at the bank and one day one of my friends from high school walked in. My Mom was helping her and said, "Don't I know you?" my friend asked, "Yeah, you're Rick's mom." Mom said, "He just got back in town." She said, "I didn't know he left." They exchanged phone numbers and Mom told me about the encounter. My friend and I had shared a locker junior year and had been friends from the first day of high school. We both had our struggles and we were down the road almost five years since we had last seen each other. College and a lifetime of experiences were behind us. After a few weeks I decided to call Melissa. We arranged to make a connection later that night. She really helped me during the time when my Grandfather was dying. I called her up to hang out with a friend. It was good to see her again. I walked in her front door and I felt like I was coming home for the first time. She was smiling big and I leaned forward and kissed her right on the teeth! True story!

She was happy to see me and I was happy to see her. It was a really nice reunion. We didn't want to separate from each other. Within a week we were making plans to move in together. Those early, carefree days of love were so wonderful. We were friends first, which really helped us. It really helps every couple. We found that we complimented each other well. We were a little leery of marriage because our parents had divorced when we were young.

We got reacquainted with each other in February and went to church together. In March I got baptized in our Lutheran church. I think it was the first adult baptism they ever did. God became even more real to me in a church setting. It seemed a little formal for me. The "Me and Jesus" days were still fresh and this was unique. I had moments during worship where I wanted to dance and it would start to overwhelm me. This was not normal in Lutheran church, but I didn't know. I didn't care. I just knew that it was fun to be with the Lord, whatever we did. This church is where I learned about the problems with American

Christianity. There was a movement to change the service to a more contemporary style. Think less organ music more guitar. There was a simple solution, do one of each kind of service. But many people dug in their heels on both sides and the church split. We lost over 100 people and many of the leaders. It was horrible. I'm sure the devil was laughing his ass off.

Most Christians have some experience with church and the challenges of it. A little bit of humility goes a long way. If we can help each other find a place of comfort where we can express our love for God in our own unique way, we will find the greatest joy ever. I have been to some churches where they dance, paint, wave worship flags, share the microphone and have discussion, not just a sermon of one person talking. It's different and I think for some people it is a place of freedom that they love. It works really well for me. There are many people who miss out on the joy of fellowship because there are too many rules and requirements in church. Jesus is not about religion or rules. He could care less about that. He would rather have a relationship with us. It serves no purpose if we learn a religious system or formula and miss out on knowing God. Pretty quickly we will start to think that we know all we need to and we won't need God anymore. We will have a system or a formula to guide us, not the King of the Universe. If we do that, we will be sorry. Many have done just that and the damage has been done. That's the church in America, guilty as charged in so many ways! Lukewarm and ineffective, but I believe it will change for the better. It has to and it will.

We were both happy to see what was before us and excited that the Lord was in it, too. One day we went to the jewelry store to look at rings. In one of my best lines ever I asked, "Do you have anything bigger?" We laughed and laughed that day. When we got married, we made it a covenant between us and God and planned for forever. We still do. We want to persevere and enjoy each day. It's never going to be perfect or easy, but if you have someone to go through it with you, you will be much richer. Every couple should decide they want to be together forever and spend their life making their partner happy. We both committed to that in the beginning. It helped that we knew each other for ten years before we got married. It's not the way most people do it, but it has worked well for us.

Onward and upward with Melissa and me! Serving each other has worked well for us. It's always fun to see the joy on her face. It's a thing of beauty and a place of refuge. After growing up with a house of horrors, it has been so restorative to my soul. We both had a similar story, our parents got divorced when we were young. We lived with the opposite gender parent and we were left to figure it out for ourselves. It wasn't the perfect way of "Leave It to Beaver", but it made us stronger individuals and able to adapt to challenging circumstances around us. We've had an amazing journey so far.

I met her when I walked into French class as a Sophomore in high school. I remember she was sitting at her desk and she was dressed in a purple and pink shirt. She kind of jumped off the page at me. God had shown me my wife, but I didn't remember that event until we had been married for over ten years. Sometimes God does really funny things to show us His heart and desire for us. I learned a long time ago, to ask Him before I make decisions related to life. You don't have to be a robot with no ideas of your own, but if you had access to the smartest person ever to ask advice from, wouldn't you ask Him? That's God! Melissa is the first person I could really attach to. She's also the first person I ever trusted. We love each other for who we are. The whole person, faults, failings, everything and it makes us stronger. It's not easy, but it's good.

I felt a pull towards many girls over the years. It wasn't just sexual attraction, it was more. There is some strange camaraderie between sexual abuse victims. Something is activated in us and we don't really understand it either, but it's there. So many times that was the case with me, some attraction mechanism was activated. It was like it wanted to drag you into something that you wanted, but at the same time it made you sick, too. It was really hard to resist, you almost feel powerless. Sometimes it was impossible. Maybe there is a spiritual component to it. It is as if there is a deposit left on your soul that draws you into an animal like reaction to a similar deposit on someone else's soul. Basically it's a curse. A literal, physical curse. I asked the Lord one time to remove it from me and I heard what sounded like velcro being ripped apart.

151

If that's you, or you think it might be, please pray for release from it right now. God can do amazing things but His ways are not our ways. He might heal you instantly, He might send you to a counselor and take some time. Don't rail against the process He has for you, it's the best way. Trust Him to lead you through it. He will get you free and more importantly help you to stay free, but it's vital that you do it His way and keep fighting. Too many of us get breakthrough, then we become passive and don't do the work of following through. To get the fullness and completeness that we're seeking we have to fight and keep fighting. It takes work to get free and sometimes it takes even more work to stay in that place of freedom. Sin and regret are wicked taskmasters, let's kick their asses and get free forever!

Chapter 28 - Lakewood Revisited
Marcus

Prison Chaplain Kelly had a friend who had a trailer in his backyard in Lakewood. He said, "I just want one person to succeed, are you that person Mr. Weaver?" I said, "You're damn right I'm that person! I am never coming back and when I go out I'm just gonna take the gospel with me everywhere." I got a letter from my parole officer, they went to look at the place and then I was out of prison just like that, after a few weeks in Sterling, parole said yes. I was back in Lakewood near the same place I lived when I was selling cocaine, crack, stolen iPods and acting crazy. I was all over that area again, but now I walked. I worked in scrap metal and it was a huge business then and I was living in his trailer. The only food I had to eat was donation type food like soups, mac and cheese, candy and bread. I had no bathroom or running water and I had only one channel on TV, the Gospel Channel. True story! I couldn't be happier though! It was me and Jesus breathing that sweet air of freedom!

I became anti-people. I was one of those who weren't fully living the new life. Just like we humans are prone to do I was going back to the old behaviors. I decided, I want to live right, so I read the Bible. I was focusing on Romans and James. Both are very powerful and books I really like. After a while of getting back into the Bible, I'm becoming better, kinder and gentler. I felt like I was walking along with Jesus Himself. It was the greatest feeling ever, and the most challenging place to stay in. Somedays, it seems like the more you want Jesus, the harder things come against you. For a long time, I never understood that it is a war. Good versus evil all day, every day! There's an enemy who hates you and wants to see you destroyed. His heart is for destruction, but Jesus' heart is for restoration. It will never change until the earth passes away. It was hard to get used to the constant battle, but once I understood it, it was so much easier to endure. If I run and try to avoid what God is doing, I only hurt myself and those around me. If I stay with God, even if it's hard, everything makes sense and works out for my good. The battle will happen either way. I started going to Church in the City and serving homeless on Wednesdays, singing in the choir and finding a real community to support me.

Then I learned all about solar energy and my plan was to start my own business. I signed up to take a class for nine weeks, but I finished it in four. It was a self-paced module of all the basics of solar energy. Mi Casa, and other local non-profits, came to the table with Dr. Elaine Smith at Charity's House. We wrote a Department of Labor grant to collaborate and we submitted it. Then six months later we got $3.6 million to start a construction school called Denver Green Jobs Initiative and it was huge! It was set up to help support the poorest neighborhoods in northeast Denver by training people for green construction and energy efficiency related jobs. Dr. Elaine was very professional and she taught me so much. She was like a Mom to me. Always loving, always supporting me, helping me heal and grow and looking toward the future optimistically. She helped me so much, to grow and be who I am. I miss her every day, she passed away a couple of years ago. She was firm, smart, wise and gentle. A real good influence on me and so many others. In my next jobs I had resources for guys to help them get jobs. For a lot of ex-offenders and others, it was hard to get jobs and that was why we had this construction school to help them.

Through Denver Green Jobs Initiative, I met Miss Eddie and Dr. Bob Woolfolk, from Agape Church in downtown Denver. We talked about faith in God and my kids and all kinds of stuff. They are still very special to me to this day. They're like wonderful parents for the whole inner city tribe, helping hundreds then and they still are today. A true lighthouse. They hosted a public meeting about a new non-profit they were trying to form a branch of. It was set up to help ex-offenders, called All of Us or None. We went to meetings and met some interesting people including each other. How cool that day was, Marcus and Rick together for the first time! Working on ways to employ the poor and ex-offenders! We went to a coffee shop and laid out the plans and dreams we had! They were amazingly similar, because we had seen it from the inside and understood what worked and what didn't. We started thinking and dreaming with an amazing team of others committed to seeing justice and mercy come forth. We formed a board of directors and we worked on banning the box that says "have you committed a crime?" on employment applications. We brainstormed how to help others re-enter society with a chance to succeed. The biggest obstacles are housing, obtaining a job, and transportation. We came up with a unique solution. A live and work space, in the same building that was close to bus or train lines. It is a good solution to the ex-offender's biggest challenges that they face. We're working on getting those properties right now. We founded a new non-profit in the midst of writing this book and this book will be a catalyst for the affordable housing piece of our non-profit, Legacy Grace Community Development Corporation. We just opened an art gallery for homeless, disabled, low income, ex-offenders and those aging out of foster care to have a place to display their art, make some sales and change their lives. They pay no upfront fee and only a 15% fee when they sell some work, where most galleries charge 50%. So many ways to make a difference giving people a hand up, with dignity.

So much to do and we like to ask each other - what are you doing to make a difference in the lives of people who can do nothing for you? How are you involving them in the process to help themselves? And what is the purpose you hope to see come forth in all of this? Our quest, our passion is to change lives. It always has been even before we could describe it perfectly. Much of the proceeds from this book will go to our community development projects. Check out the back of this book for more information about it. We have offers in and we're negotiating for properties. We're looking at buildings all the time, trying to find funding sources and exploring all of our options. Helping the world is a big job. We believe helping one person is a huge job. People are messy, they need friendship, time, love, kindness, direction, healing, sometimes a kick in the butt and so much more. Working with others is successful when we are welcomed into their lives and really start to help them change themselves. Real change is internal not external. That's why throwing money at the problems of social ills or trying to only change behavior does not work. We have to help people change the way they think, get to the root issues of struggle and repair them. Only then can lasting change come forward.

In many ways, I think that black people are worse off than we were fifty years ago. So many ways. Yes, we got our civil rights, but we didn't lose our slave mentality. Many still think we're back in the cotton fields or worse, with no way out. Many have abandoned their families and forsaken marriages in record numbers. Almost 70% of our children are born of wedlock in America. When we were slaves we sang songs of joy to our creator about his deliverance and mercy towards us, trusting Him to come through. Now we are free and we sing about sex, drugs and crime. We have little purity, less hope and no sense of direction. We have allowed our culture to take us away from our place of honor and our new found land of promise and prosperity and put us into a new type of bondage. Public welfare programs are not helping us. They are keeping us in captivity. Sure it's nice that President Obama wants to give us a free phone and food stamps to help to pay the bills, but it comes at a price. We have forfeited our nobility in exchange for a welfare that keeps us alive but kills our souls inside. Think about it.

Our prisons are full of men and women who have no fathers, no direction and little hope. This is supposed to be our shining moment, an ever improving pathway to restore all that was stolen from us so long ago. Look at our Native American brothers, their men are aimless, they have no purpose. Many warriors and braves sit around drinking themselves to death because they have lost what once was theirs. A passion for life, a proud purpose in it and believing that the Great Spirit would help them on the journey. They, like us, have had their dignity, passion and essence dismantled and destroyed by a culture bent on keeping them down.

It is time to stop this madness once and for all. The only way we will have true joy and fulfillment is to get back to being good people. We can't go to the clubs every night and leave our kids to fend for themselves. We can't have sex so easy that kids are born in poverty and disgrace where there's no commitment. We can't bitch and moan about our situations, then rob stores for money. We have to change into who we really are. America will die without us. We are the conquerors, we are the heroes. Why do you think we went through all the crap that we did? The one who suffers and endures to the end is the one who wins in

156

the end. It's the central message of Jesus. He suffered and died so we could live. Not so we could watch porn, do drugs and eat government cheese! Why don't we start living! Our country is in deep trouble and if we don't get excited about fixing this mess it will be too late. I will tell you something about the political arena. We are pawns in it. Now it's set up as an excuse to take our money and our children's money. We have nearly $20 trillion in debt for the United States, half of that was added during the last eight years under President Obama, but it's not just his fault, it's all of our leaders who have lost their way. That's about $65,000 per person for all 300 million people living in the U.S. now. What happens when the debt comes due? Are we going to give them all of our National Parks to pay it? Or are we going to go deeper into bondage like during the great famine in Joseph's time (Genesis 47) and give all our possessions, land and finally our own freedom just so we can eat, to despotic and tyrannical rulers? Are we?

If someone bent on our destruction controls the food and water supply, we will all be slaves again. Black, White, Latino, Asian, poor, rich, it won't matter. Many of the environmental programs are now geared toward making us grow certain crops or eat certain meat. Cattle take a lot more water to bring to market than chicken or pork, for example. That's why we're heading to a point where beef could be outlawed because of this. Tomatoes take more water than most vegetables to grow. Pretty soon, you will need a permit to grow tomatoes or it will be outlawed altogether. Does that sound like freedom to you? That kind of scenario is lining up all over the world. Politicians are arranging circumstances so we will be reliant on the government or another entity to survive and eventually we will have to give everything to be able to eat. Take a look around. None of the political players have our best interests at heart. Maybe Donald Trump will make a difference, it's early yet. We really need him and so many others to free us from this scenario. It will take unity, sacrifice and more to return America to greatness and freedom. It's time to pray for sure!

Our Congress, for example, has a separate system for their healthcare, not the one we use. They get a lifetime salary after one term and are wined and dined by special interest groups and lobbyists ad nauseam. It's a good system when it's run with real integrity, but nobody is playing by the rules anymore. Almost nothing important gets done and all our people suffer for it. It's time for a radical change. Some political people are corrupt. Their focus is on sexual favors, drugs, alcohol, bribes, taking advantage of people, putting us into economic bondage and not enforcing the law. That makes a corrupt society and it will be devastated, even destroyed if it doesn't change. Think Anthony Weiner. The religious people don't advocate for the truth anymore, they say, "It's okay, God will forgive you." No He will not. If you know something is wrong and do it anyway, that is sin. Sin leads to death and hell if you're not careful! Some of the pastors who are supposed to lead and care for people are so caught up in being celebrities with rock music shows, a huge following and popular TV shows that they are forgetting God altogether. They may use His name, but their hearts are far from Him. They have gone their own way and God is not amused by their worship of money or celebrity status.

There are radical problems with our political system now, it's not about helping others or making real changes, it's about a few people getting rich off the system and selling the rest of us as slaves. Maybe it's time to start over and get back to doing it the right way. Yes Donald Trump is an arrogant guy and has some issues, but he has been elected President and now is the time for all of us to come together in unity and work together to fix this country. What a mess it is. It will take all of us, our skill and talent, our ability to work together and humble ourselves to do something remarkable and save America. It will take all of us!

Men, we are the heroes! Come forth men and women, it's time to rise up! What America needs now are some men who understand hardship and suffering to rise up and restore what America can be. What we were as a nation. We're not perfect, but we're better than this. We can endure the suffering, the ridicule and we have the strength to outlast, overcome and walk this whole mess into freedom! We can do it, but we have to get serious about our calling and destiny. So far we're believing the lies about us and not changing the world. Come on black men of valor, rise up, be a husband, be a father, be a good soldier, pray and ask God to help you. Cover each other in prayer so we can do it. Jesus already won the victory, all we have to do is occupy it! Who else can do it? It's up to us now! We've got to become the Navy Seals of our generation and liberate the people of America from evil, sin, slavery, guilt, sorrow and shame. We were brought here from Africa for a purpose, and that time is now! Just like the Israelites lived 400 years in bondage in Egypt, we have lived in slavery all over the world for about 400 years, too. It's time to come forth, to gather together and ask the Lord for His way and direction. The victory is His and we can join His elite forces and change the world for good so let's do it! We have been allowed to suffer, we have been chosen to forgive and we must embrace it and do the mighty acts available of us. It's challenging, but it's worth it! We already have the fortitude, the power and ability inside us to be mighty and to bring lasting changes. Let's bring America back from the edge!

Here's a good example of where we are. We haven't even taken a stand against human trafficking yet. We should be dedicating tons of money, volunteer hours, resources and more to that cause. If anyone understands the horror of it, we do, yet we sit idly by and watch the world make slavery a top priority again. We know better, yet we do nothing. The shame that is heaped upon us, is our own fault if we don't respond to it, defeat it and make some changes. We get correction so we can get back on track. Have we lost our minds completely? It's time to stay out of the clubs and the strip bars, get clean from drugs and alcohol. I know this life is tough, but get tougher. Save money and send a kid to college or trade school, quit gambling and smoking pot and use the money to help a mom afford to pay daycare for her kids. It's not that hard and we have to try, time is running out! People are getting rich from the slave trade and we sit and watch TV and play Xbox. Are there any men of valor left ready to fight a worthy fight against injustice? Any William Wilberforce's out there? Or Frederick Douglas's? Or Winston Churchill's? No one knows how or when it's all going to go down, but the book of Revelation is pretty clear, it's going to get ugly as the end draws near. Jesus said it Himself. It doesn't feel that far away. The end times will be marked by rampant racism that occurs. It's happening right now. Maybe it is intentional from the powers that be. It's hard to deny what is happening all around us. Take a look.

Revelation 18:7 Nation (ethnicity) will rise against nation (ethnicity), and kingdom against kingdom. There will be famines and earthquakes in various places.

We are seeing these events begin. If we don't wake up, it will be too late! All that was done to us in evil will be returned onto the heads of those who did it to us! It is a sure promise from God, let's confess our faults, laziness and weakness and ask for His wisdom, strength and endurance. He has all that we need and He put it all inside us in Jesus. Once we say yes, we can do incredible things with God! It's not rules, regulations or performance, that's religion! It's knowing God, doing the right things with joy and doing it with God, in His timing and His way. That is the kingdom of God! We have His permission and His power to overcome the world and now is the time! If we are passive and commit no energy, urgency or resources to change the situation, we alone are to blame! Rise up and be mighty, black men of courage! All men of courage! Native American men of courage! Latino men of courage! Asian men of courage! White men of courage! Rise up! What if we worked together in unity? We could change the world and everything in it, in one generation. Our children would be free to think, dream, feel, paint, make new music and dance! That would be a good heritage to leave them. What do you say! Our unity is one of our greatest strengths. We need to be intentional to work as a team and win! It's all before us. We have a lot of work to do. Let's do it!

Chapter 29 - Going to Prison
Rick

Hiding things is easy when you're dysfunctional. You become an expert at it. The Lord is not fooled by whatever it is you think you're getting by on. He sees it all. So one day He asked me, "How about prison ministry?" I said, "How about forget it?" Then He asked me again about seven years later. I said, "Is that what you want me to do?" Notice the difference in my answers? Apparently I needed seven years of maturing before I could do something remarkable. As I understood it, the idea was to stay out of prison, not to go there voluntarily. Then I met a guy John at church who happened to do prison ministry at Denver County Jail in addition to being a professional Santa Claus. So I went with a group just to check it out one Sunday. We went into an eating area with giant metal tables anchored to the floor. Think industrial cafeteria. You could barely squeeze into the seat. It was not built for beauty or comfort. This was the work release area of Denver County Jail and many guys were close to getting out. They were working jobs to prepare for the transition back into real life. They paid a hefty rent for the privilege of working all day and sleeping overnight in jail.

Prison is a very interesting industry to be sure. It seems less about the rehabilitation and more about the confinement now. Increasingly, it's becoming a for-profit model and that means there is little or no incentive to help guys get out and stay out. They are a commodity and a source of income to be gathered, not a person to be helped. It's a strange metamorphosis that's occurring more and more. Rehabilitation is not the goal anymore. So the five of us are standing there looking at each other. I said, "I'm ready to go with a message if none of you are." Everyone nodded and I went ahead. I had a good knowledge of the Bible, good notes and most importantly, the Holy Spirit. When you have the Holy Spirit, you are always in the majority with His majesty. There were about 25 guys in the service. A heckler tried to get me off topic, but I turned it back on him and asked him some deep questions. After a bit he left. He just wanted to argue but something changed when he did leave. When the meeting was over there were four new believers in Jesus. God had decided it was their day and He used me to help them get there. I was hooked! I liked evangelism and I liked hanging out with God. He sure goes to some funny places with funny people like me! A taste of spiritual warfare and watching God's love in action.

I started going to do services in jail twice a month, then four times a month. I wasn't going to church, I was bringing the church inside the walls. I started fasting and praying, getting better prepared to teach. I spent twenty or more hours a week studying the Bible, seeking answers, making solid points and clearer presentations. Then something funny began to happen. When I put down my Bible and started speaking from my heart, the whole room would change. The Holy Spirit would manifest and it was powerful. I was way off the notes now and making a connection to the guys in ways I never knew before. One time I fasted for twelve days before I came in to teach. This was to the hard core guys in Building 22. They were coming from the top level security units in Colorado. Murderers, rapists, armed robbers, and more. I came in and shared from my heart from the beginning. I talked about the long fast I was on, about smelling frying bacon the day before, it was nuts. I told them I fasted and then I blasted them with this truth: all I did for God is nothing compared to what I've done against Him. Look at my pile of filthy rags ten feet tall all the way to Albuquerque (from Denver)! I was on fire and they were cut to the heart. Fifteen guys came to receive Jesus that day. This one dude, Dwayne, he was about 6'5" and 290, solid muscle, he came forward crying like baby and said, "I want Jesus!" We prayed and praised God. Only Jesus could turn a room full of hardened and broken criminals into a room full of mighty warriors for Him. He gets all the credit, all the glory for whatever has happened in prison and elsewhere. I have helped lead maybe 1000 people to Christ there over the years, but it's all Him, not me. It's His call that they answer, not mine. It's His love that changes them.

One time, the veil was very thin between heaven and earth as I prepared the message for the week. I was seeing things and understanding like never before and I was given some kind of prophetic

162

insight. It was kind of freaky when my boss grew claws and fangs right in front of me. It was crazy and I got away from that job soon after. I think it was a warning. This is the same guy who asked me to falsify official documents and was corrupt in every way.

When we came into the work release cafeteria room for our service that Sunday, there were demons scratching on the windows trying to get in. I talked about how Jesus fulfilled so many Old Testament prophecies and I went through it pretty methodically. I gave the altar call and the whole room came forward to receive Christ or to pray with the guys who did. My co-minister and friend Jack still talks about it! Only Jesus could do that. He is worthy to receive glory, honor and praise. I could do nothing without Him. I take no credit for it, I just point to Him as the author and finisher of our faith. He is good and His mercy endures forever. That's why we can be different. That's why I am different. And why you can be different. He is why we can overcome the horrible life we were given, choose to forgive and make a difference from now on. It's why we do what we do.

People always ask me if I'm scared going to prison. Honestly, I felt like I was safe the first time and every time since then. I could be worried, but I'm not. Even when we went to the Limon Correctional Facility and they did a full swat tactical inspection of every car, everything we had and all our volunteers. That was wild, but we had no fear at all. They had 40 armed officers, plenty of firepower. It was almost two hours before we were allowed to come in and do a yard event with 300 or so lifers. Limon has about 2400 guys under lock and it's an interesting place to say the least. Most of the guys are never getting out. We had such an amazing service there, it was epic. Full joy coming forth. We had a large band playing rock music and they let us bring in food and they never do that. It was God's favor, plain and simple.

Another time, this kid about 19 years old came into the room for a Bible study, maybe ten of us were in there. He was physically ill. I was alert to him instantly. I prayed and asked him if it was his first day in prison, it was his second day. Ray, my co-minister, and I started talking about fathers and the guys got antsy, it was hitting home. About 90% of the guys in prison have little or no relationship with their fathers. I basically had no father either. Ray shared about what it was like to be an African-American in America for his father's generation. For the black men in the 1940s, it was a way different world, being held in contempt as some kind of animals. Being treated poorly and never being respected as men. We forget sometimes what dads and grandpas went through in the 20th Century. Trying to bite their tongues to keep the peace when everything inside of them wanted to attack and destroy. The inmates were getting killed emotionally as we went on, then a miracle happened. I said something like this to the guys: "I'll be your father. I'm sorry I hurt you, son. I was unable, unwilling to help you and I'm sorry. You are special and I want to bless you. You have what it takes already inside you to succeed. You don't need to be afraid or let circumstances steal your joy. Let me go, son, and step into your destiny. You can be a good father, a good husband; I bless you with the fullness of life, peace and joy. You can make it, son, it's already inside you. Let me go and walk into freedom!"

You could have heard a pin drop. The entire room was weeping, even me. I had found my calling, my destiny. I was a father to the fatherless. I have five sons and they're all adopted. All are very social, all different and I love them deeply. They have helped me grow and stretched my limits. Each one is a blessing, tell your kids today that they are a blessing if you haven't yet. Go tell someone else's kids. It needs to be heard, for all of us. Everyone is special, everyone is important. No one should be safe from a word of encouragement, a hug or a blessing! We have love to share and we need to in a pure and sweet way! I've mentored well over a 100 kids so far. I call them my kids. Most have had hard life stories like mine. Not perfect or easy, but they have come through. Life is a process every day and it's worth the work it will take to get you there. Even if it's hard. When you get freedom that lasts and understanding that guides and protects you, you will see the value of working through the process. It will be great! Sometimes life comes disguised as difficulty, but it's really a chance to help you be who you are.

Chapter 30 - Life on the Outside
Marcus

Life after prison is building and rebuilding, learning how to live in the world with all the requirements, challenges, choices and temptations. Sometimes being in prison is easy, it's a chance to listen, study and pray without all the other distractions of life. I know that sounds weird, but it's true. Once you get out and there is freedom, girls, work and time commitments, life gets harder. It seems like your friends will be waiting for you with drugs, alcohol and girls when you get out of prison, sometimes literally at the gate. Most of the time no one is there waiting with some encouragement and a commitment to help you stay successful. Something is wrong with that picture, don't you think?

After Denver Green Jobs I found another place to learn and grow called Bud's Warehouse, where I was the General Manager. It is a home improvement warehouse for donated items in remodeling or construction. It was a place of new beginnings. Most employers didn't want to hire a felon right out of prison, but there were some that didn't mind being the second employer. It's a mindset we had to learn and use to our clients' advantage. It's a key in all we do now. Our program at Bud's gave them a job to work in the warehouse and a chance to get back on track. They had to want to change. It was ideal, some structure, physical work and a supportive environment. It let them interact with people and find their place in a new world where they had all the decisions again. It can be very scary to have freedom after you're told what to do all day every day for years while incarcerated. Many people get overwhelmed by that part alone! Some go back to prison quickly because of the struggle and the stress. Managing life is challenging when you have to learn it all over again.

Life on the outside can be difficult and many just give up trying to get it all done, to make the appointments, and do all that is required of them to stay out of prison. The system requires a lot and many times it is too much, especially if you're traveling by bus lines and trying to work a job. It seems set up to make them fail on purpose. It is very difficult to succeed in that scenario. It may be time to refine and revise the requirements of parole to make it possible to complete the process. No one wants to see unrepentant, dangerous people on the streets, but we need to give them a chance to make it, don't you agree? Everybody deserves a second chance. I'm glad I got one. More like a thousand second chances. I refuse to allow anyone to treat me like I was once treated.

Marriage is a weird concept to me. I was raised as there was basically no value in it. The level of commitment modeled was superficial. With the level of dysfunction I endured, it's still hard to connect with people. I can put on a good show and maybe you will believe I'm okay, but on the inside I'm usually not. I'm trying, but I still get nervous around people and I still have trouble attaching to anyone emotionally. It's a constant process, even today. Learning by doing. It's the school of hard knocks. Christ is with me and opening up doors for me. I love Him deeply, but I still feel restless in my spirit on days. There's always more to the story I think. When I left prison, I cried and cried. I was so happy to get out and so sorry to leave the guys behind. They had become my family and I had started to feel very close to them. It was a new feeling in my life. A real family. Out here in the real world, everyone was busy and we might hang out, but it wasn't the same level of friendship, fellowship and closeness. I needed my brothers and they were doing time. I think some of them needed me. It was never quite as simple as I expected it to be.

We started having meetings at Bud's Warehouse where we had leaders and para church guys from all over the city come and share ideas about how we could work together to bring jobs to felons, provide housing and services around them and change many lives. I was so excited for the possibilities. I met so many amazing people and we talked about a lot of great things. Some good came out of it, but it seemed like talking is all we really got accomplished. How can we do more than talk about the issues and problems? We had plenty of good ideas. We shared fellowship and wisdom. It was a good time. It wasn't all that it could have been. I think sometimes as leaders we are too cautious about what we do and try to control it perfectly. God is not afraid or cautious. He's

166

the King of the Universe. Life with Him is a little messier than that. Of course, we have to operate with wisdom and good stewardship, but sometimes God wants us to go ahead, even if we don't know where we're going. Even if we don't have all the answers yet. We don't have to do it perfect, the Bible is full of guys who messed it up and God still used them. The light is always green with Him and when it needs to be red, He will let us know. That's a little different mindset, but He is committed to us doing His work and bringing His kingdom to earth and it's not usually in ways that we would do it. He's too creative to do it with a formula or a script. He would rather be interesting and creative, not boring and predictable. It's funny because He never changes, but He uses His creativity in endless ways. I love sunsets and I'm amazed how every day, every single one is different. There's subtle ones and powerful ones that take your breath away. I never get tired of the beauty that He makes. Each one of us is a beauty! He sees how wonderful we are, and He made us gorgeously! He is committed to us and He loves us! He will never stop encouraging, teaching, guiding, loving and showing us what to do! He loves it and He is fully committed to us being amazing and complete! Like every perfect sunset that takes our breath away!

Jeremiah 29:11 For I know the plans that I have for you declares the Lord, plans for your welfare and not calamity, to give you a future and a hope.

Chapter 31 - The Future
Rick

I never finished college, but I always could get a job. Having a strong back will do that. If you can do a job that doesn't require you to do manual labor, I would recommend it. Later on it will matter. When you're 25, you can hammer away all day, but those years of hard work will come back later and make you wish you had finished your degree. Be serious about your future, you may not finish when you're 22, but it's important to get your education. You don't want to be doing day labor at sixty years old trying to make a living with no retirement. It's not a good scenario and one that too many people have chosen or allowed to happen. I think the days of working for one company for forty years and retiring are long over. It's going to take an entrepreneurial spirit to make a way for our futures. We will have to invest in real estate, businesses and other cash flow entities that make consistent incomes and offer some safety and security. It seems like waiting for a retirement or Social Security may be pipe dreams at this point. We need to be smarter and plan differently than our parents did. We have to be diligent and focused in all we do. We are planning for a good future and are committed to it.

God promises us a good future and a hope if we will trust Him. He loves you and He is waiting for you to come home. It's a different way of being, but He wants to love us and have a close and powerful relationship with us. Only He can do that, and He wants too! He is a good God and you can trust Him. Really, you can! He will put you in the middle of a cause and make a way for you to have an effect. Here is one he has put us into.

In Wisconsin there were 600,000 deer hunting licenses issued and no one was killed by hunters. It's important to see the gun control debate for what it is. It's an attempt by some to try and control the access to handguns and other weapons. I think for mental health reasons, it would be good if we were really intentional. Maybe we could require a mental health exam before someone could purchase a weapon. That sounds crazy, but most of the people who have been involved with these mass shootings have mental health issues. Maybe we all do. Perhaps instead of banning them outright, we could find a way to screen out the unstable and untreated ones so we don't have these shootings. It may be impossible, but banning all weapons is not the answer either. Then the government or foreign powers could come in and take us over with very little resistance. That's what the Second Amendment is for, to protect the people from the government and foreigners bent on our destruction.

I hope people realize that evil exists. Sometimes it comes in disguise, but it is everywhere. Religious people are not evil as a group but some are and that's true of most subgroups. Former military, college students, high school students and the unemployed are not inherently evil groups, but some people within them are. We have to be careful not to lump everyone together in one group and call them all evil, it's not true and it's unrealistic to do that. Political correctness tries to do just that. We need to be sure to remember that everyone is capable of evil, it is part of our human potential. We need to be wise enough to say the truth and not generalize or make up our own truth. People stopped having honest debates. We have become immature people who argue and then shout down anyone who doesn't agree with us. It's a terrible excuse for journalism, politics, maturity or civics in general. Yet it's allowed to happen. It's a desire to control people and it needs to stop. There is no wisdom in this kind of behavior. Our debates used to make us stronger. It opened us up to other points of view, it made us think and not just parrot someone else's ideas as our own. Democracy is only useful when all opinions are allowed to be expressed, even the wrong ones, even the ones we disagree with. Defending someone else's right to be a bigot or stupid is foundational in America, but the political correctness movement is trying to squelch us all. We need to talk it out like we used to. That's where violence decreases. If I talk to you, I might understand your perspective. I don't have to like it, but you look through different lenses than I do. It helps me see and maybe I can help you see, too. It's easy, and it works!

I used to say, "I may hate what you say, but I will fight to the death you're right to express it." People are more like marshmallows now. Taking a stand for something, especially someone else's right to be a moron or to be rude is becoming unheard of. It used to be different in America. Now we are wimps and lacking backbone, virtue, fortitude and many values that once made us great. Maybe the Trump election changed some of that. Our enemies are winning if they are turning us into selfish people, caring only about ourselves, wasting our time and money on the wrong things and running away from our good moral foundations at lightning speed. Look around, is anyone trying to be wonderfully selfless anymore? Or are we just making money, spending our time on shallow pursuits and using our talents to help ourselves and not others? I think we need to make some changes, and we can, it's not too late. It's time to say what's wrong and fix the mess.

We don't have to be politically correct anymore. We can be honest and polite and should not have to worry about being attacked. It's like we were in a trance of something and nobody could say anything about anything. Well, we're not in a trance now! Let's wake up out of our slumber, out of our apathy and laziness and do something that matters again. After the September 11 attacks of 2001, thousands of men and women joined the military to fight for our country and defend this great expression of liberty called America. Many died and paid the price for that privilege. Many more were maimed and disabled for life from their service. They know what it's like to humble yourself and do something for someone else. We honor and salute you for your courage, your selflessness and your commitment to keeping America the land of the free. You are the heroes, and you may be the only ones left. Rise up so we can thank you and show us the way to be excellent again. I think maybe we forgot. Thank you for your service! Please help us get back on track! We need a few good warriors to help us get there and right the wrongs.

Chapter 32 – Dignity

Our circumstances have been bizarre, but we have gotten to help so many people get their lives back on track. Somedays we almost feel like the heroes that we've been talking about. Whether helping people get jobs or finding somebody a place to live, it's an adventure and a privilege to help others. Part of the process is helping ourselves to overcome what we went through by helping another. We spent years doing that, and maybe even in some unhealthy ways because of what we were processing. Helping people get their self-respect back is not doing everything for them, it is helping them see that they have potential and they can be someone. They just have to believe it. We help them find their own way. It works! A lot of people just need to get a little wisdom, sometimes just someone to listen is enough. It's been a challenge to balance it and a privilege to help them walk through it and we love seeing the positive results. It gives you hope in the battle when someone gets it and moves ahead. Even if they struggle, they're trying and that makes all the difference. It's the same story: a job, housing and transportation are the three keys. We believe we can make a huge difference, not by raising taxes and making more laws and programs to help people, but by helping them help themselves. They know what they want to do, where they want to go in life. Sometimes, they just need a little assistance getting there. There have been so many governments and organizations who have made a career out of trying to create programs to help people which have ended up only putting them into further bondage. It takes away their incentive, creativity and passion to become who they are. Let's dream and encourage others to do so, too.

In our country, we have done that to some people. They get a factory job, a warehouse job or maybe a government job and it's a living and it is money, but it slowly kills their joy. I think that making less money and loving what you do is more important than anything. Especially for men who find so much of their identity tied up in what they do for work. It's extremely important that it be something they love and are passionate about. I'm not saying quit your job today and run off into the fullness of irresponsibility with wild abandon. You can do that, but it's better to have a plan. Have some money saved up and make a plan before you walk in and tell your boss to take this job and shove it.

It would be helpful to have the whole picture in front of us. Do what you can. Pay your child support, make arrangements to pay off your past due debts and credit cards, get a job right away, but always be looking for other opportunities to better yourself. Be proactive! So many men are not encouraged to pursue passion and it's one of the main reasons why we are so inept, bored out of our minds and painfully unhappy. Sir Richard Branson has done amazing things in unconventional ways. He started companies and has lived a life of adventure. Branson has dyslexia and had poor academic performance as a student, and on his last day at school, his headmaster told him he would either end up in prison or become a millionaire. That sounds like most of us really. Plenty of opportunity for both extremes inside us humans. The point is to figure out who you are, make a plan and go after it. Branson started his empire in a church basement selling discount records by mail order. Now he's a multi-billionaire. Anything is possible, you just have to believe, give yourself a chance and start doing the right things. Your destiny is waiting for you to line up with it.

Having kids will change your life forever. I wonder why we are so flippant about it, as if it's not really that important somehow. When I was a kid, I didn't appreciate that mindset toward us. Children are a wonderful gift from God. He alone decided the time of our birth and who we are. There is one egg in the womb available to be fertilized, and millions of sperm swimming there to try and get in. In that moment, God is there creating the new child. Before He brings the child into the world He knows them intimately. Before the sperm and the egg come together, the Lord is there in that moment. He is loving us and intimately acquainted with us, even before the moment of conception. He chooses the exact sperm from among the millions to make us. He knows who we are before we are made in the womb, before we're born, live our life or die. If He knows you and me fully and He made us for a purpose, so there's a pretty good chance that He has the best info for the path we should follow. It's important to seek Him in little things and huge life decisions. His heart is for us and not against us, so everything He does is going to be for our benefit and for His glory. It won't be easy though and that can be confusing at times.

He will allow things in our lives to make us and mold us into who He made us to be. We can be immature at times and think that the process will be easy. Most likely, it will have some degree of difficulty and may take a long time for it to be accomplished. Anything worthwhile takes effort and perseverance. God does not usually work in our lives like a light switch. He won't just flip a switch and we become a marvelous person, with plenty of money, great relationships, perfect hair and minty fresh breath. The process He takes us through is for teaching us new ways of thinking and acting; of seeing things and people like He does. It's not about being negative, offended or wounded anymore. It's about overcoming the things that have happened so you can be all that you were made to be. God doesn't value us based on our behavior. He loves us completely and totally already. He knows what we've done and

175

what we're capable of. That is true, unconditional love. If God only loved us when we behaved perfectly, I doubt He would ever love us at all. I know He wouldn't love me based on my performance.

So we each have five children and what an interesting journey that has been and still is. Each one is so different, some are adopted, some are step kids and some are biologicals. Its way cooler the way God did it for us. Each of these kids has a plan and a purpose over their lives and God knew it from before they were conceived. The same is true with each of us, we are filled with a plan and a purpose, designed for greatness and victory. Since that's true, it might be helpful if we engaged God to find out what that plan and purpose is. I would hate to get to the end of my life and find that I had missed it completely.

Some of our children have been through tremendously horrible things and some have been born in a car on the highway. True story! I was trying to drive my wife Megan to the hospital to give birth to our daughter, but there wasn't enough time even though I was doing about 100 miles per hour! Maggie was born in the car on the highway and she was perfectly healthy. We think she might like to go fast, do things quickly and become a wonder right before our eyes. She may love to travel, she may have a heart for nursing. The possibilities are exciting! She was a promise fulfilled and she is perfect, and wonderfully made. She is a representation of restoring things in my life, things I didn't understand were still missing. Suddenly I could be a father, I could be a daddy, and the redemption is real for me. God was affirming me to be fully who I was made to be. She is the gift that keeps on giving. I just have to participate, be thankful and keep moving forward. I let each of my kids down in the process of learning what was important. I've hardly seen two of my sons who live elsewhere and I'm sorry for what I've missed in their lives. I want us to be closer. We don't want our kids to go seventeen or twenty-two years between visits with their dads like we did.

I understand it all differently now. When I was running my game, I didn't want to be a father or a dad. Just like the example of my fathers before me I didn't think I had to be one. In my culture nobody was being one. I was playing around and I hurt my kids in ways I never imagined. They could have a father and a daddy. It took me a long time

176

to realize what was important. It took forever to grow up, to believe I could do it, to recognize that my kids mattered more than my fear or my failures. I didn't know how to be a dad. It's hard to come back into their lives after many years, but it was worth it to try. I can be in their lives at whatever level is possible. It is so messy to try to repair a relationship, but I finally learned to forgive myself for leaving them behind. They got some of my drama and they did nothing wrong. It breaks my heart. I have no excuses. I chose myself first and my kids had to bear the load. I want to help them. I have sent them letters, I have re-connected and I would like to encourage all of you to try. You can't be a father over night, but you can have a conversation. Tell them you're sorry. You don't have to be perfect, but you do have to be present.

Now be prepared, it might not be easy at first. Kids and moms might say horrible things to you or about you. Fair or not. They might make it tough. Understand that you did wrong by your kids and you have a lot to make up for. They need you, no matter what they say. If you don't try you will regret it and your kids will hate you forever and it will be harsh as you sit around someday lamenting the mistakes you made. It sucks growing old and no one wants to see you anymore. Restoring a relationship, it's better than self-medicating your pain away, running the streets or hating yourself. We can go for the gusto and have sex with every girl we meet and watch the carnage pile up, or we can find instant gratification by being there for our kids.

Chapter 34 – Adoption
Rick

My wife and I could not conceive. We got pregnant a couple of times and could not bring to birth. Then we tried to adopt a child from a private agency and found that process to be painful in so many ways. We felt like used car salesmen trying to convince some scared girl to pick us as a family for her unborn child. When they told us to borrow someone's dog for our family picture, because expectant moms like dogs, we were done. Honesty is important to us, so that didn't fly well at all. We were sad and feeling lonely, getting older and with no children. It was a place of wounding for us. We decided to start a weekly home group on Thursday nights to avoid the despair that had arrived to devour us. It was important for our sanity, but something else happened. We began to have hope.

We were at risk of missing out on one of the greatest blessings of our lives and giving up on our dreams. Maybe that has happened to someone you know. Situations and circumstances make life challenging, even arduous at times. It's at that time, in that moment, when you have to decide who you are going to be. Are you only going to believe in good things when life is good? Or will you expect the best no matter what is happening around you? Maybe this has happened to you, too. We had a watershed moment. We could stay depressed and sad or we could believe in the great life that was available to us if we didn't give up. We chose life! So we went to an informational meeting for adopting a child through our local county. It was a brutal process. The first thing they do is show you a photo collage of some of the most horrific child abuse that has ever happened to kids. We all cried in the room. At least half the people left and never came back. We dug in our heels and said, "Let's do this." We found a new place of tenacity, but it wasn't activated until we stood up against the sorrow, the past history, the expectation of gloom and doom. That's how this life works. If you want it to be different, it's up to you to change it. You can't usually snap your fingers and be transformed, but you can decide to start the process that fast. Then you can seek the Lord and ask for His help. You can read books and do it your own way, but I learned it takes a lot longer and costs a lot more to do things my way.

So we got through the process to be certified as foster parents (required for adoption) and got matched with a little girl. She was wonderful and we started the transition to have her as a foster child until the adoption was final, usually within a year. We had visited her a couple of times and were ready to take her for an overnight to our house. Within a week or so kids transition to you full-time. Then she would stay with us forever. Something happened, that we never expected, on the way to having a daughter. The foster family that had her had fostered 38 children and never adopted one of them. This time was unique. Once we came, they realized that they couldn't let this sweet girl go. They wanted her and they needed her. Here we were entering another moment to bleed. So they kept her and it was the right thing for sure, but that didn't make it easy. We had to feel a depth of heartbreak that miscarriage never took us to. We cried and cried. It was a devastating blow to us.

It turned out to be the perfect fit for her. She was a year old and they were bonded. It was so right. We got to suffer for her good. Without us, her parents didn't know they couldn't let her go. With us they did the right thing and we got to get killed emotionally for it. It's a little bit like what Jesus did for us. He suffered horrendously for our good. A total self-sacrifice to pay for our sin and shame. That's what our lives are supposed to be like. It's not about filling up our own tank with every desire. It's about looking around and seeing what we can do to help someone else fulfill their desires and destiny. Of course we can have fun, but there is much more than this narcissistic version of life where our own pleasure is the only priority. Our culture needs to adjust. Certainly something to consider. This was in July. We needed to take a break from the intensely emotional situation. We were ready to try again in a couple of months. We had heard about a little boy and were very vulnerable and emotional, but the idea of a baby for Christmas was a great hope to us.

We waited for a call that never came. It was weird. Thanksgiving came and went. Christmas, too. We were cut wide open. It was so hard to wait and not know if this could really happen. We could have given up, but we were not getting beaten. Beaten down maybe, but not beaten. We got a phone call near the end of January, six full months later. It was about the same little boy. We were excited, but cautious. It's hard to be hammered that many times and not start questioning if you're doing the right thing. Maybe we missed it. You don't get to meet the kids before you say yes to having them. They tell you what they know and give you time to answer. Talk about going on faith. We said yes! It was all arranged to meet him in a couple of days. We were sitting in our truck outside the foster parents' house and I looked at my wife and said, "This is how you'll know it's from God. We're going to go in there and I'm going to say his name and if he lights up like a Christmas tree, you'll know it's from God." So we went in. He was six months old and laying on the floor and I walked over to him. He was a chubby little fellow. I said his name. Samuel wiggled and smiled and reached up to me. He knew his daddy's voice. Praise God! Melissa picked him up and held him and he fell asleep on her, a beautiful confirmation to her. We took him home to stay a few days later, but the test was still to come.

After we had him for a while, I was holding him one night and he wiggled and I dropped him. He cried a little, but it seemed like he was okay. He rested and was content. The next day I was moving his legs trying to exercise him a bit since he was chubby. It seemed like he was having some pain from one particular movement. I was concerned maybe something had happened from the fall. I took him to the hospital and told them the story. When they found out he was a foster child, they immediately called social services. They came in and interviewed me. A police officer did, too. There was a risk we could lose our son, and I could go to jail for child abuse. The process was playing out, another chance to have hope in the midst of the storm. I was focusing on God, not on the circumstances. It was tough. In the end they let us keep him. He had a tiny buckle fracture. They put him in a cast for two weeks. Our next challenge was, he has a Native American background, so we had to see if the tribe would adopt him as one of their own. They have the right of first refusal for tribal kids before an adoption. His birth mom was never registered with the tribe so they had no claim on him.

His leg has been fine ever since. We were finally able to complete the adoption about a year later. We stood before the judge and we finally had a son! What an adventure it all was. He is such a treasure and a blessing. He's the son I dedicated this book to. My number one. He is my son and I love him so much. It was such a process to get him. Bringing a baby into your marriage after twelve years was a big adjustment, but it was worth it. Every second of it! The pain, the sorrow, the wondering. God used it all for our best and He will for you!

Chapter 35 - Perfect Chameleon

There was never a time when I felt comfortable in my skin. I was always the tall one, the weird one, the goofball, the playboy. You name it. That was me. Trying to fit in, a perfect chameleon within every group, every sub culture and every place of sorrow. Creating another personality was necessary, even helpful for surviving the onslaught. There was always plenty of shame and regret to be found in the lives we were given. See, when your heart is broken, you will do almost anything to make it stop hurting or to fill it with something else, even for a while, to give you some relief. There was tons of drugs and alcohol, those are easy. Sex goes a long way, too, as do pornography, money, cars, fame, greed, all of it. Looking for something to fill that void is an endless search, because nothing will ever do it except Jesus. The other things will hide the pain for a minute, but they can never take it away. There is something rotten in it, as you try to cover the awful things, all you do is add more garbage to it. So you not only have the original problem, you have something more. It's a vicious wheel of misfortune spinning you into places and things that you just can't understand. It's like one day you wake up and say, "How did I get here?" Most of us don't wake up one day and say, "Hey I think I'll become a serial killer today!" It's a process of little choices over time. If you choose to get healing you will avoid a lot of the other choices.

Ted Bundy was a good example of that. He had been into pornography and little by little he went deeper and deeper into it. There was control and power available to him there and he saw it as an exploration. He had a single parent mom and a grandfather who acted like a father to him. His grandfather was into porn and was sometimes a violent man. Bundy was an anomaly in many ways. He was not raised in a life of great instability or abuse that many of us have suffered. He became more withdrawn in high school, plagued by immaturity. His isolation was fueled in the sexually themed real life detective novels he found in the trash near his house.

In the spring of 1966, he met Stephanie, the love of his life. She had beautiful dark hair and a great smile. As the time went by, she grew bored with him. She felt he was too childish and immature and his tendency toward manipulation had ruined the relationship. He soon dropped out of Stanford University upset and brokenhearted. The following fall he entered the University of Washington with renewed fervor. He went from an average student to an honor student. He became politically active and he met Liz, a divorced mother of a three year old. It looked like they were going to get married. Ted was accepted into the University of Utah Law School and within a few months was murdering women at an alarming rate. Over two dozen were murdered during his reign of terror. What caused a nice looking, outgoing honor student to become an FBI Top Ten Most Wanted List fugitive kidnapper and murderer? Ironically, Ted Bundy worked at a suicide hotline crisis center in college. He tried to save lives for those who were hurting deeply, yet he took many lives, too. How can that be?

Are we just as capable as he was to do incredible acts of mercy and goodness and horrible acts of murder and mayhem? The answer is yes. Each of us has great kindness and goodness in us, but we also have a great capacity for evil and chaos. Is it really true? Yes it is and I have a few theories why. Most of us have life experiences that are either good or not. The truth is, most people travel a similar path. We may have had a different kind of abuse, neglect or shame inflicted upon us, but most people have had some level of it. No one's story is without some pain and suffering. This is in no way to diminish what any of us have gone through. Each heart receives sorrow differently and processes the offenses in unique ways. Your process is important and how you deal with your pain will ultimately determine who you are and who you will become in some ways. It is never easy to travel that road to healing, but you can do it and there are many others who will help you! Just don't be a victim like we were. Spending our time and effort being a victim and not getting healed almost cost us our lives, but we learned that there was more to us than being run over by life, there was hope. There is hope! Ted Bundy said in his final interview with James Dobson that he was not physically, sexually or emotionally abused. I've taken some excerpts from their conversation the day before he was executed.

In it he says:

"It was a fine home I grew up in, good parents and a life for all of us six kids. I encountered what I call, soft core pornography at the grocery store, magazines of pretty girls in various stages of undress or swimsuits. We boys would find provocative books in the trash or old real life detective magazines with sexually explicit and violent stories. I am not blaming pornography for what I did. I take full responsibility for what I've done, but the issue is how this kind of literature helped mold and shape the kinds of violent behavior I did. It fueled fantasies and created an almost separate entity within me. After a while, I had gone as far as I could with the literature and an interest was sparked to go farther, to do a physical event. It happened in stages gradually. With pornography, as with any addiction, you keep looking for, craving something harder (to keep the excitement level up). You reach a jumping off point, where maybe doing it for real would do the trick. I was there at that point, for a couple of years. I had been taught against violence and criminal behavior at home and in school. The last vestiges of restraint were tested and fueled by the pornography. It became a compulsion, a destructive energy released and my control and restraint was eased with alcohol use. I don't know why I was vulnerable to it, but I obviously was. That was central in the violent behavior I engaged in. After the first murder, it was like coming out of some horrible trance, to have been possessed by something so horrible and to remember what happened. Worst of all the realization that in the eyes of the law and of God, I'm responsible, I'm guilty. I was absolutely horrified that I was capable of doing something like that. I was conditioned that this was wrong behavior but my repeated indulging in the fantasy of sexual violence started to become stronger to where I couldn't control it anymore. It became a compulsive type of sexual frenzy. It was an unbridled passion that overwhelmed what I had been taught as a child. The two things were at war with each other inside me. After the first time killing, the release of energy receded so I was myself again. Basically I was a normal person, I wasn't a bum or a pervert, I wasn't hanging out in bars. I kept this part of myself well-

185

hidden where even friends and family had no clue. Once I was arrested, they were shocked. My basic humanity was intact, but it was overwhelmed sometimes by this thing. Pornography can reach in and snatch a kid out of any house today, no matter how diligent my parents were, there's no protection against the kinds of influences that are loose in the society that tolerates it. I haven't done a survey, I mean, I don't pretend that I know what John Q. Citizens think about this. But I've lived in prison for a long time now, and I've met a lot of men who were motivated to commit violence, just like me. And without exception, every one of them was deeply involved in pornography, without question, without exception, deeply influenced and consumed by an addiction to pornography. There's no question about it. The FBI's own study on serial homicide shows that the most common interest among serial killers is pornography.

Well, I know it would have been a far better life without pornography. Excuse me for being so self-centered here, it would have been a lot better for me and for a lot of other people, I know that, lots of innocent other people, both victims and families. I know that people will accuse me of being self-serving, but we're beyond that now. I'm just telling you how I feel, but through God's help, I've been able to come to the point where I feel the hurt and the pain that I am responsible for. Yes absolutely! In the past few days, myself and a number of investigators have been talking about unsolved cases, murders that I was involved in. It's hard to talk about all these years after because it revives in me all these terrible feelings, and those thoughts that I have steadfastly and diligently dealt with. And I think successfully with the love of God. Yet it's reopened and I feel and I felt the horror again and all that I did. I can only hope that those who I have harmed, those to whom I have caused so much grief, even if they don't believe my expression of sorrow, and remorse will believe what I'm saying now. That there are loose in their towns and in their communities people, like me today, whose dangerous impulses are being fueled, day in and day out by violence in the media in its various forms, particularly the sexualized violence. Let's come into the present now, because what I'm talking about happened twenty or thirty years ago, in my formative stages. And what scares me, Dr.

Dobson, is when I see what's on cable T.V. Some of the movies, I mean, some of the violence in the movies that come into homes today, stuff that they wouldn't show in X-rated adult theaters 30 years ago.

I'm telling you from personal experience, the most graphic violence on screen, it gets into the home to children when they'll be unattended or unaware. They may be like Ted Bundy who has that vulnerability, that predisposition to be influenced by that kind of behavior. Influenced by that kind of movie, by that kind of violence. There are kids sitting out there, switching the TV dial around and come upon these movies late at night, or I don't know when they're on, but they're on! And they keep watching. It's scary when I think what would have happened to me if I had seen them. That was scary enough! Well I just ran to stuff outside the home, but to know that children are watching that kind of thing today, or pick up their phone, and dial away for it or send away for it, it's horrible. That desensitization process, I'd describe it in specific terms in that each time I'd harm someone, each time I killed someone there had been an enormous amount, especially at first, an enormous amount of horror, guilt and remorse afterwards. Then that impulse to do it again would come back even stronger. Now, believe me, the unique thing about how this worked, Dr. Dobson, is that I still felt, in my regular life, the full range of guilt and remorse about other things and regret, but this was compartmentalized. It was a very well-focused, very sharply focused area where it was like a black hole. You know, it was like a crack, and everything that fell on that crack just disappeared.

I can't begin to understand the pain that the parents of these children that I have, and these young women that I have harmed feel. And I can't restore anything. I won't pretend to, and I don't even expect them to forgive me. I'm not asking for it. That kind of forgiveness is of God; if they have it, they have it, and if they don't, maybe they'll find it someday. I'll answer really honestly. I don't want to die; I won't kid you. I can't kid you now! I deserve, certainly, the most extreme punishment society has. I think society deserves to be protected from me and from others like me. That's for sure. What I hope will come of our discussion is I think society deserves to be protected from itself. Because, as we have been talking, there are forces loose in this country, particularly, this kind of violent pornography. On the one hand, well-meaning decent people will condemn the behavior of a Ted Bundy while they're walking past a magazine rack full of the very kinds of things that send young kids down the road to be Ted Bundys. That's the irony. We're talking here, not just about morals, what I'm talking about is to go beyond retribution. Which is what people want with me. Going beyond retribution and punishment. Because there is no way in the world that killing me is going to restore those beautiful children to their parents and correct and soothe the pain. But I'll tell you: there are lots of other kids playing in streets around this country today who are going to be dead tomorrow, and the next day, and the next day and the next month, because other young people are reading the kinds of things and seeing the kinds of things that are available in the media today." Dr. Dobson said, "Yet you told me last night (and I have heard this through our mutual friend, John Tanner) that you have accepted the forgiveness of Jesus Christ and are a follower and believer in Him. Do you draw strength from that, as you approach these final hours?" Bundy replied, "I do. I can't say that being in the Valley of the Shadow of Death is something I've become all that accustomed to, and that I'm strong and nothing's bothering me. Listen, it's no fun. It gets kind of lonely, and yet I have to remind myself that every one of us will go through this someday in one way or another. It's appointed unto man. Countless millions who have walked this earth before us have gone through this, so this is an experience which we all share."

Ted Bundy was executed a few hours later. What could be more horrible than what Ted did? Is there anything worse than the savagery he unleashed on the world? Yet the Hitlers, the Moussolinis, the Idi Amins, the Saddam Husseins, the Caesars and Neros, the ruthless Americans killing black slaves or Native Americans, have been non-stop in their existence on earth and will be here forever. Ever since Cain killed Abel it's been a slippery slope. There is no lack of brutal, selfish, vile behavior in this country or any other. So why are we surprised? Evil is real and it's here to stay and there is only one antidote. The blood of Jesus Christ is necessary to eradicate sin, shame and suffering off this planet. Without Him we are left to destroy each other in whatever fit of rage, control or lust we create. With Him there is hope and forgiveness, a peace like no other and the ability to salvage a life filled with tragedy and turn it into good. Without Him we are puppets to be manipulated into doing all the evil that we are capable of. With Him we can choose something better. Once you look honestly into yourself and remember all that you've done wrong, it can be a heavy and painful experience. Go further and ask the Lord to show you what you're capable of. I did that once and vomited from the depth of depravity. Our capacity for evil is staggering! Things that Ted Bundy did, maybe worse.

In that place of awfulness, I heard the Lord say, "Even if you did that, I would still love you!" That is true love. Love conquers all and it can never be defeated. God is love. Let Him love you and fix what is lacking or missing in your heart. He is good and He will help you if you ask Him to. No matter what you've done. Confess it and ask Him to forgive you. Jesus was chosen to forgive and He had to suffer to do it. His death brings us life and makes a way for us. I say, "Lord Jesus I have made a mess of things and I need you. Please forgive me for all I've done wrong: every thought, word and action. Please forgive my sin and teach me your ways so I can follow you and be free. Make my days have purpose and my heart have peace, Amen." I love you Jesus!

Chapter 36 - Theater 9
Marcus

I discovered you just have to be real and that's exactly what I did. I wanted to help everyone with everything I could. I wanted to help people find jobs, affordable housing and self-respect. In my experience, the best remedy is employment first, and housing is a close second. I ended up doing a lot of case management, too because the guys needed it so much. Over time I became known in the city. I met a lot of people with the same heart to do the same things. To help the homeless, ex-offenders and marginalized to find their dignity and get their lives back on track. I am a total community guy doing board service, being a community resource and an asset to several non-profits. I had to learn to wait, to pray about things more and not react so quickly. I changed jobs a lot and when it was time to leave it was always a steppingstone to the next thing I was learning. I joined networking groups, made connections and was appointed to the Mayors Workforce Investment Board. I spent a lot of time investing in relationships and helping people connect the dots. The at-risk adult was finally becoming who I was always supposed to be. Then came July 20, 2012, when my life changed forever.

A new girl had come into my life through my blog "Many Parts of the Body." I gravitated towards her. She had people of trust and others abuse her. It was a familiar refrain. Pretty bad abuse. We became instant friends. We had that similar story and when you find someone who understands the insanity, you can become close very quickly. Her name is Rebecca. We had a lot in common. She wanted to help people, too. I think it was us trying to help others as a way to help ourselves heal. Somehow being nice or learning compassion are the byproducts of a life gone crazy.

I remember I had taken vacation from work on the 19th to look for a new apartment and we had breakfast that morning. We had talked about going to the new Batman movie. I said, "I want to go, and you should go with me." Her answer was yes! That day she reminded me about getting tickets in advance. So I got two sets of tickets one for that night and one for the next day. I needed the Batman movie for a distraction. He is one of my very favorite characters to enjoy. I came back around 11 o'clock p.m. and put my stuff down into some seats. Usually as I'm walking in, the police are right there but they weren't that night for some reason. At this theater complex, the gangs would sometimes show up, so security was usually tight to keep the drama down. I walked into the theater lobby and it was busy. Premier night of The Dark Knight Rises. There are people in costumes everywhere, but no security! Weird I thought. I was excited, new movie, new friend and she's a beautiful girl who really understands me. Maybe something special was coming. I was excited and I met her out front and got her a hot dog and a soda.

We're walking into theater nine. I got in the middle section and see my friend Kaylan. I know her from Church in the City. She was a younger girl and I didn't want to say anything to her since her friends were with her. She was three rows in front of me with her cousin Ashley. It reminded me of people I had to give up at Church in the City. I missed singing in the choir and serving the homeless in the park on Wednesday nights. I missed the relationships with people who were real and who had overcome a lot. I was a resource for many people to find jobs there. A lot of our congregation was inner city folks with various issues: being homeless, poor, uneducated or with health issues. It is a wonderful place, a real family. Rebecca calls me back into reality with a tug on my sleeve. We were happy like little kids. Her smile lifted my heart. We took our seats. Fifth row center, perfect spot. I love the movies. It has always been a place where I could think and dream or have an escape from life. I was so excited!

The movie was about to start when a smoke bomb suddenly went off. I'm like, what the heck! There were strict fire restrictions that summer, fireworks had been cancelled statewide and I couldn't believe somebody did that. Some prankster I thought, but it was not a joke because the light came on. You can see the movie start playing, the shooter's silhouette down front and you can see the lights. A lot of people were in costumes, so it didn't register at first. I could see the silhouette of his gun and then he started shooting. I can't tell you how weird it looked. This guy is in a helmet and had a full commando outfit on. He's just shooting randomly and methodically from the front of the theater. Where am I? Wake up! But this is no dream, it's a nightmare.

It is stadium style seating and the gun barrel moves up and down in no particular order. There's a light flashing in the gun muzzle every time he squeezes the trigger and there's a green laser for targeting. It is so loud it hurts your ears, it was so surreal, I'm sitting in the fifth row and I'm in shock. I can smell the gunpowder. I can feel the severity of hatred and evil intent coming forth. I try to get down as well as I can. I just wait and pray and pray and pray. You can hear the bullets whizzing by your head. The projectiles hit targets easily. How did I get to this moment in my life where I'm being shot at by a random stranger in a theater? Maybe Rebecca got in front of me to protect me. Everything just happened so quickly. What if I sat in the right seat and she sat in the left? Would I be dead instead of her? So many questions. So I get down almost on the ground and her movement is stopped. What always got to me was people jumping on you, knocking you over or stepping on you to get out of theater. Just running down the middle aisle screaming and trying to get out. The survival instinct was strong. None of us were thinking about neutralizing the shooter, we just wanted to live. Human behavior is very interesting to me. Some people had training or were strong, but everyone wanted to live first and foremost.

I heard a voice in my head as clear as day say to me, "When he stops shooting, leave the theater." I thought, "Hell no, I'm not going anywhere! I am way too big. I'm going to get killed if I move!" He ceased shooting about 20 to 30 seconds later. When his gun jammed it was like a stampede to the door. People tripping over each other, it was absolute chaos. I got Rebecca up but I can't get her out. She was limp and bodies and people were everywhere crashing into each other, trying to get out of there. It was a game of Twister with blood, chaos and gunpowder thrown in. We were still in the theater, and then he started shooting again. He began with a shotgun I think that's why I got shot in my arm trying to get her out. She fell right back to where she was sitting. I was trampled over and got shot in my leg but the bullet went through and then I went out the exit and went outside. It was total pandemonium.

193

A cruel scene of carnage, confusion and craziness. There were people and blood everywhere. It was ghastly and insane. I still can't believe it was real. A little girl told me I was bleeding. I didn't even feel it. I was shot in my arm and my leg. My mind was racing. I wanted to puke. My knees were weak. What happened? Where was Rebecca? Was she okay? What about Kaylan? Oh my God!

I was doing all these great things for God but I never really gave God the credit he deserved. He saved my life that night and I give Him all the credit. He has always been good to me, better than I deserved. Things like me getting a shorter prison sentence, the mentoring from all the guys I'm still friends with. Meeting Dr. Elaine, who was a mom, a role model and a mentor to me. If it wasn't for those people in my life and many more, I'm not sure I would be here today. We need each other. I'm just surviving on the miracles of God every day. There were about ten bullet holes in my theater seat. How did I survive? There were police and medical staff everywhere after the shooting. There was snarled traffic, it was absolute anarchy everywhere. It was like a movie scene. No one was buying a ticket to this one. Where was Rebecca, did she get out? Was she still alive? I couldn't breathe. The first voice message I heard was a call from my Mom. She left a message and I didn't realize the depth of everything that happened until after the hospital trip. I knew people were shot, but I didn't know how bad it really was. It was a massacre. The city was quiet and the sun was out. I go to my house in a daze. There are people with cameras and they stop me in my front yard when they interviewed me. I didn't want to be interviewed. Oh God, I didn't want to go back to the theater again and tell my story, but my friend, she's nowhere to be found. I was getting deeply concerned. I'm only one person, I tried, but I couldn't pull her out. What was happening? My anxiety and guilt were off the charts.

After the interviews with CNN, ABC, NBC and all the others who were set up across the road I was so fried. It was July 20th. It was a media frenzy. When I first said I forgive the shooter, people didn't like me. They thought I was stupid, a liar or that I wanted to be famous. I understand it like this, I forgive and I forgave him, because I need the most forgiveness myself. It's easy when you understand that. I went through a lot, but I put others through a lot, too. You understand forgiveness when you have blown up other people's lives and I am so sorry for what I did. No matter what happened to me that was no excuse for making a mess of everyone else's life. I need forgiveness first and foremost. Just like Herb did, just like Holmes did. We all need forgiveness and to forgive others.

I had a guy that taught me a long time ago when I was down at my lowest point to keep my head up no matter what. Now I was at my lowest point again. I heard that some had died and I'm already up over 24 hours straight. I was hanging with Rebecca early in the morning on the 19th and we went to breakfast then she went to work for a while. Then I'm up all day on the 19th and into the next day and it's time for those interviews again. It got to me, I didn't have anything left, I was so beat up physically and emotionally. The exhaustion, the pain, the anger, oh man! There's all this insanity and excitement going on around me. God gave me the words, I said, "I forgive the shooter. Of course I will, it's what my faith teaches me to do." But somehow it's what I had to do. Faith declares it, but you confirm your faith when you live by it, no matter the circumstances.

One media guy asked me, "Do you believe in the death penalty?" I said, "Vengeance is the Lord's!" Someone else asked me, "Would you really forgive the shooter?" I said, "Yes. I lived with my stepdad, who did a hundred times worse things to me. I couldn't forgive him for so long because there was so much pain in my life. He's way worse than the shooter ever was or could be. All he did was shoot me in my arm." The media guys lost it. They were falling all over themselves. They said, "Oh shit, what's your name?" They started listening to my whole story. It's not just about the shooting, that was just a part of it, it's about how do you forgive? I never expected to be a spokesperson for forgiveness, but it found me. I just opened my mouth and incredible words of healing could came forth. It was God. He was using all the years of abuse, sorrow, shame, fear and regret to make something beautiful out of my life and for others to see it was possible. I'm not self-promoting, God can use anybody, but he chose me to forgive and is using me as a light to make a difference in the world. Only He could bring me this far. I never wanted or expected it. I never believed it was possible, but here I am.

I get invited by this group called Friends First to speak to kids in middle school. I had the ultimate testimony now as an Aurora Theater survivor. I started speaking around Denver at schools and prisons and I am granted the freedom to share my whole story. I've come a long way but I stop and give all the credit to God. Otherwise, you start screwing it up. If you think it's you, it becomes a mess. So I refused to do that and I always gave God the credit everywhere I went. Pride comes before a fall, and I've had enough of those for a lifetime already.

The reporters were reporting it everywhere, after the shooting, when I gave God the praise! I was bold, but I had broken through something. I never felt this level of peace and joy and at the same time, I'm feeling an incredible loss. Rebecca is dead. I cared for her deeply and my heart is crushed and broken. She had dreams to help kids, we talked about what we would do to help the kids who are like we were. So much good could have come of it, and now it was over. I had powerful feelings of love, respect and guilt. Why did I survive and she didn't? So many others were maimed way worse than me. Twelve people lost their lives, their families are destroyed and their lives ruined. I just got shot in the arm. It was inspiring and crippling, all at the same time. It was a heaviness in my soul that was ripping me apart. I just wanted to breathe and it was hard to. Four years later, it still is.

Things keep getting added into my life and I'm getting on a helicopter with the Mayor of Aurora Steve Hogan. I was the only victim that goes up and I got to meet Denver Mayor Michael Hancock, too. We're still friends today. So we went up in the front of the helicopter and we took off. We prayed over the Aurora Theater. It looked strangely serene up there. From above you see the symmetry of a city. You don't see the challenges, the graffiti, the people in need, the stories of hope or pain, it all looks pretty well together. When you get down to street level is where you see the needs, the challenges and the stories of real life. That's the place I live in. That's the world I dwell in. Where people need help. I'm there, because it's where I'm supposed to be. It's where Rebecca and I were meant to be. When you overcome the kind of things

196

that we did, you're likely called to help others. Being chosen to forgive is something you have to embrace or it can destroy you. That's why we need God here to help us or it would swallow us whole and spit out our bones.

Talking about the theater still bothers me, it's painful to remember and re-live it. It took a long time to even decide to co-write this with Rick, knowing the trauma and heartache it would bring. It has, for both of us. Digging up our past again and reliving all this junk has been an onslaught and an emotional minefield. So why do it? If we can help people live in freedom, walk out forgiveness or get released from their past, then it's worth it. There are laws in place for child abuse and the things that we went through and we thank God for that. In those days, it was a joke. It's important to talk about hard things when it helps people. No matter what it costs us. My stomach used to hurt during the drama, now it hurts again for a world heading off the rails at high speed. Life is not easy, I guess we have to get tougher to survive. These days are not easy. As I'm writing this there's a news report about a mass shooting in Orlando on June 12, 2016. There are 49 dead, 53 injured. Oh man, it's all coming forth. Evil is no joke and it's time for good people to get tough. The bad guys are committed to our destruction, so we better be committed to doing the right things and helping people get free. The war is on. I had the fight or flight mechanism activated for a long time in my life to protect myself. Now it's trying for more moments in my life again. It's hard and it makes me want to retreat on days, but I can't do that. I don't want to be afraid anymore and I won't, it's the only way I can be successful. We win if we show up, it's that simple. So let's show up. If we don't, we're finished. I'm not kidding.

Chapter 37 – Aftermath
Marcus

The reports are absolutely awful: 12 people are dead, over 70 injured. I am taking morphine for the pain in my body, but there's nothing for the pain in my soul. I'm getting calls from national and local media, so much so that my phone died. People from around the world sought me out. Overnight I became a pseudo celebrity and a reluctant spokesman for the victims. I know some people hated me for it, the anti-gun advocates did and Jesus haters. There were many people who didn't like all the attention I was getting. I'm not sure I liked it. It was hard to deal with. It kept everything fresh in my mind, going over things again and again was painful. The trauma of the theater shooting lasted forever. No one would let it die! It was difficult, interesting, agonizing and much more. The media was relentless. The trauma of the theatre shooting kept replaying in my mind, the sounds, the screams and the realness of it all still causes me nightmares today. God surrounded me with His love and walked me through the worst desert imaginable and He won't let me go.

The Lord kept sending people my way to teach them grace, mercy and forgiveness. He had to teach me, too. It was a chance to give God the glory and show His power for restoration. That's the only reason I kept doing it, because it was hurting me to live in it all the time. One thing that's hard to grasp is how talking about a trauma keeps it fresh in your mind. You don't get to start processing it when you're still reliving it constantly. It delays the natural pacing of event processing. Some of you know what I mean. It's PTSD. There is a traumatic event that happens and the anxiety and the flashbacks of that event can be a source of pain and suffering for long periods of time. It can be events of violence, assault or tragedy. It can be mental or physical. I had no idea what was going on for a long time. I was drifting, like a ghost or a cartoon character. I couldn't think. I couldn't sleep. I couldn't stop crying alone. The aftermath was hard to deal with. My life became complex amidst the circus surrounding that night for years to come. I was trying to move forward but I was not taking care of myself. I was refusing any medication that my doctors offered. I felt like they were trying to fix me by making me into a zombie.

I have a deep respect for Megan Sharp. She came back into my life one night. It was my first night out since the shooting. I thought of when we met that day long ago serving food to the less fortunate at Wednesday night meal at Church in the City. We served along with her son and Kaylan who was also inside the Aurora Theater. I just wanted to get out of the house, it had been so long and my friends had arranged a night out to go Karaoke, one of my favorite things to, do before the shooting. Big Hank, my stage name for the past 25 years, wanted to do karaoke and guess who was there, Megan and we became closer friends. My friends really liked her. Sounds like God had me right where He wanted me. She's a strong follower of Christ. I really liked her style, her smile and I felt like a king. She was my queen and beautiful, inside and out. I got her number that night and we set a date up for later. I told her about the baby on the way with another woman, and she was okay with the situation. Eventually, she heard all my stories, all the drama, all the regrets and she never hated me or judged me for it, she just supported me, loved me and helped me fix it. Not all women are that way. That takes a special person. She is my all. We started dating about two months after the theater shooting. She was amazingly kind to me and her son became my son, too. Both of them were always ready to talk to me about the ten million things going through my head. Megan was a God send, a gift from heaven. I knew she was the one after a date on the town at our first concert. We walked all the way to and from the concert hand in hand. She is a rock for me to lean on, a precious flower. We dated for a while and we were married in March of 2013. She is a sweet gift to me from God Himself. We had a private wedding at City Park that snowy day. The best thing I have ever done.

Look around and be thankful for what you have and who you are. All the little things, they matter. Not what you don't have or what has happened before. Focus on the now. It's the present, the gift that is today, each moment, savor it, live it like it matters. It does. Gratitude makes life better, fuller, richer. Try it out. Trust me, you will not be disappointed. This is my Wife's DNA, and it became mine, too. Mitchell, her son, was protective and just wanted his Mom to be loved. With the theater shooting backdrop, blending all of us was hard. I never took into consideration that it was just Mitchell and Megan for a long time. Then here I come, this guy, all of a sudden with this crazy story and a painful past. Mitchell questioned me about my kids and I tried to answer honestly, but usually it was not enough. He wanted to see if I could be trusted. Would I be around for the long haul? He was right to ask.

My mind was racing most of the time, but I would still go to work every day at Bud's Warehouse. Helping people wasn't enough and after a while, I couldn't take it anymore. Something was wrong with me. Really wrong, but I was too afraid to admit it. I told Megan one day, I feel weird inside. I have a sadness, a sense of impending doom. It's irrational, it's overwhelming and it's real. I don't know what to do. I told Megan what I was feeling and she and my lawyer Phil suggested a talk with a counselor. I was still hearing the thunder in my ears every day. The shooting wouldn't stop. It wouldn't go away. The loss of Rebecca was such a struggle. The guilt and the anger were so fresh for so long. The counselor wasn't helping much so I went back to people who had helped me through difficult things before. I spent time with Tammie at New Genesis, with Miss Eddy at Charity's House, Anna at Denver Works and friends I knew before the shooting. They helped me a lot when I was getting my life together off the streets from years earlier. I spent time volunteering, trying to find solace in the lifting up of others as I had done dozens of times before. It's a way of life for many victims of abuse. Trying to make up for the abuse by being compassionate or kind. It's a strange by product of a life gone horribly wrong. I still thought I could do everything. I was in physical pain and had outbursts of emotion frequently.

I felt very insecure in public and would always sit in the most defensible position and locate the exits, anywhere I went. I would only go to a few places that I knew. I did threat assessment and watched everyone closely. I became reclusive and I still do at times. I was determined not to see a therapist for treatment. Like most African-Americans, we think people only see therapists because they are crazy. I was working for a guy doing scrap metal and mentoring people again.

George has an infectious positive way about him. He never let you get down for long. He really helped me through some difficult days. He had a vision for helping the homeless, too, so we became great friends. I felt bad complaining about shoulder numbness when others have lost their lives or live in wheelchairs. I was thankful to be alive. The guilt of that is a tidal wave crashing down on you constantly. I stopped talking to my wife about the shooting for a while. I kept seeing story after story of Sandy Hook and other shootings. Then I would see my face on every network or in print. Talk about a challenging time, but I'm still trying to move forward. One day is the midst of this funk, I decided to get off the couch and go to the movies. I went by myself and I picked the film American Sniper. I saw myself in Bradley Cooper's character. I was distant, suffering from PTSD and it was clear. I decided to take care of my mental health. I asked my wife, "How do you see me?" After she affirmed what I knew and some consulting with Phil and his team, I decided to start my recovery. I had to get better. I became a client and I was determined to dive in. I worked really hard with my therapist and my wife and I'm finally at a point where I'm moving forward. Jennifer is a great therapist, she and Dr. GQ helped me get back on track with medication and learning the art of processing things. I had to stop everything for a while and just breathe. She helped me do that with each session and with my frequent talks with Megan. I also had a great network of people around me who were awesome and supportive. Those are the necessities for healing. Be proactive, it will really help!

Then I was offered a radio show with George. You don't make big money, but you get the notoriety of it. It was KJHM 101.5 FM. They never give you a radio show like that, but they did! It was God again, making a way. I needed a guy like him because George would not let you feel down for even one day. His energy level was so high that to keep up with him was difficult. He invited me to his office and we talked about a lot of things and he was impressed. He offered me a job the next day doing metal scrapping and mentoring. The clouds were clearing some.

Then I was offered a job as director of client services at New Genesis and I also worked part-time doing development and coaching with Denver Works. I get to work with men and women every day that were like me ten years ago. It's crazy and amazing! They look up to you for being a guy that overcame all these huge obstacles. I teach resume building and have booklets of jobs and housing for people in need. I help people navigate the system and build their confidence, dignity and a road to self-sufficiency. I help them do it, but they still have to want to. New Genesis was a tool for helping me become a better person when I first got out of prison. This was well before the shooting. After the shooting they helped me, too. I hope to inspire the current residents that with God's help, a person can overcome anything and everything. Integrity is important to me, so I try to instill it in them. Doing the things the right way is paramount to growing up and getting ahead.

Me and my son, Jamin, started having a better relationship. I was in Iowa many years ago, and his Mama got pregnant the first night we slept together. We didn't really expect or mean for it to happen. She left town when she got pregnant and she told me she's having a baby and I said, "fine, whatever." I was so caught up in myself then. I realized when my son was born, I let him down. I loved myself more than him in that moment, and I was wrong. So now he calls me and I want to rise up to be there and help him as much as I can. Sometimes, I don't hear from him for a while and I know he's going through it. I know what is going on, I've done it all, too. It's hard to watch your kids struggle with the same things you did but there is always hope.

When they re-opened the theater, we were all invited. I went back and forth on the idea, but in the end I went. I was shell-shocked being at the theater again, we walked through the lobby and I'm hyperventilating. I wanted to run. The emotion hit me like a charging rhino! Full speed! I'm walking to Theater 9 which now is called Theater H. I had asked Megan and Kaylan, "If I go to the theater, will you go, too?" They both said yes. We prayed for peace. People asked me, "Why would you want to go back?" Ultimately, it was because I wanted to say goodbye to my friend, Rebecca. I felt like doing that in a personal way, asking her to forgive me was the right thing to do. Her spirit was there. She was waiting to love me and forgive me. She never felt like she needed to forgive me, but I did. It was another moment of God giving me the best He could. Now I was chosen to forgive myself. That may have been the hardest forgiveness ever given. I let her down and she died. I should have protected her. Rebecca would have none of it, she was letting me off the hook. She was giving me her love and forgiveness. Now I needed to agree with her and let myself go free, too. It was so rich and so ugly. The most stirring example ever to me of the paradox of this life. I cried in a new way, tears of joy and deep lament.

They were showing "The Lord of the Rings" that afternoon and I sat near the company big wigs. It was weird. I saw many of the victims, people I had met at court or the hospital. Some of them were in terrible shape. We would just like to thank the first responders and all who helped us, without them, many more of us would not have survived. The theater company, Cinemark, needs to improve their security measures and take responsibility for what happened in some way. Twelve people died, 70 injured, a whole community shattered. It wasn't all their fault, but they dropped the ball big time and people were killed and wounded. The shooter should have never been able to leave the door open, go out and come back in like that. Door alarms are standard in theaters and retail outlets almost everywhere. When someone moves through the doorway it rings or something. It is tragedy upon tragedy. As we entered the theater, there is little girl standing there with her mom and it was Kaylan! She gave me the biggest hug. I just started bawling because I'm so happy to see her. I'm happy after all she went through that she had made it out. We sat together. It was so very weird and strangely therapeutic, too. I wanted to run out that door screaming, but something made me sit there and stay there. Jesus was with me, otherwise I'm out.

A while later, George and I are going to churches, prisons and jails to talk about Jesus. Then we took it on the road to Tennessee and Virginia, too. Around Thanksgiving after the shooting Channel 10 did an interview at my old childhood house in Virginia Beach about the shooter and my Dad. Herb saw it on TV that night and I was scheduled to leave early the next morning by plane. The phone rang and that was Herb who called and my Mom hung up on him. My Mom and I are on the way to the airport early, like 4 o'clock, and she says, "That call last night, it was your daddy wanting to say he was sorry." I was just shocked and overwhelmed! Wow! God is powerful, a Mighty King, A Good Father and I am overwhelmed by His goodness! Only God could change Herb from a megalomaniac into a humble man asking for forgiveness after years of separation. It didn't mean I wanted to hang out, but it helped me on the journey. I hope it helps him, too. I was gravitating to teachings about the power of forgiveness and so it became a theme of mine in my talks and speaking engagements. I talk about forgiving in this way: this is not about what happened, the other person or what was done. It's about you being able to let that thing go and move on. Sometimes it's forgiving that person for hurting you, sometimes it's forgiving God for allowing it to happen when He could have prevented it. Sometimes it's forgiving yourself for not being tough, smart or strong enough to resist or overcome it. Forgiveness is key. Without it we are reckless, dangerous and spiteful. With it we have room to grow, mend and rise into a new way of feeling and living. A whole new expression and a place of joy are waiting for us if we will embrace it. Who can we forgive right now?

Chapter 38 - Trial by Fire
Marcus

George and I went to back to Tennessee to visit more prisons and minister there in and around Nashville. It was a great feeling and a precursor of bigger things to come. It's good to be just visiting and not a full time resident. It's the first time I was ever brought in and let out on the same day! We were on death row one time and these guys that are never getting out of there, they are praising the Lord like I have never seen. I would never be able to go into a place like that if not for the shooting, my own rebellion and being willing to go when the chance came. The Lord endorses His vessels that He uses. A warden saw us on a TV news story and invited us to come to Murfreesboro. They were doing stories on us everywhere. I didn't even realize what I was doing at the time. I can't open up these doors for speaking engagements, it was God totally behind it. I was staying really busy and I was alienating my wife by doing it. I was gone a lot, but she supported me. She missed me, but I was afraid if I stopped, I might crash and burn from the stress. If I started thinking about July 20 again, it would be bad, real bad. My anger, rage, guilt, sorrow, angst and more were still raging and I was running.

Megan, Mitchell and I went to speak at my friend Lin's church in North Carolina. We went to the mall and they had a praise dance team and a worship band. I spoke at the mall about my story and two girls, who were sisters, and not speaking for almost their whole lives, made up when they heard my message about forgiveness. They were in tears as we all prayed together and praised the Lord. We bring the fragrance of heaven and the Lord is pleased when we do. I have seen miracle after miracle happen. At first it was hard, but the more I was honest and transparent the more people would be moved to forgive someone or to be forgiven. People accepted Jesus Christ in droves and it reminds all believers of our calling. A little faith is the Lord's intent. Here I am, Marcus Weaver, seed planter, motivational speaker and someone who has seen the power of true forgiveness. I've come along way. Is that why

He let me walk out of the theater? Is that why He let you escape some horrible situation, so you could be light and life to someone else?

Sometimes I wish it was me and not Rebecca who died. I'm trying to live on with her good legacy intact. She had a great heart, she overcame a lot. She taught me to let things go in a way I never could before. She was my friend and I miss her. I ponder it a lot. She was my helper at a critical moment, even to giving her own life. She was chosen to die that I might live. That others might live or come back to life again. I found it so rewarding and so excruciating in so many ways. She was chosen to forgive, then chosen to die. I was chosen to forgive and then chosen to live. I still ask God why. He seems silent most of the time, but every once in a while I hear Him whisper, "You are my gift to a dead and dying world." It's He who chooses us for His plans and purposes. It's up to us to live out the path He has chosen. He knows it all. It won't always make sense or delight us, but He can be trusted and He will make something beautiful out of the strain.

That gift was revealed in a new lease on life and a closer bond with Jesus. Those tears brought Megan to wipe them and push me to be who I am in Christ. I'm at my daughter Maggie's doctor's appointment and I see my Megan in her face. My grandmother who just passed away, I also see in her face. I see my own mother in her face and I see every girl that I ever liked, loved or took advantage of. She is a great redemption for me. A calling me up higher gift from God. A sweet innocent girl who loves me for who I am and forgives me for not getting her to the hospital on time. She just turned one year old. What grace and life she is to me. I don't know everything but I'm learning. God gave me a little girl so I could be a good daddy, be hands on and so he could continue the process of healing my heart. She helped me forgive myself for my past failures with my boys. I'm still a work in progress just trying to be transparent and real.

There's still more to do, farther to go, but He is with me. My wife and my daughter are with me. My other four children are with me at various levels. Restoration has come and it is coming. I'm rejoicing and expressing gratitude. My life has purpose now and positive effect in so many ways. I think there is no excuse not to be a father. It is the single most important thing that you can do as a man, and the hardest challenge I ever have faced. I wrote each of my sons letters, years ago, expressing my deepest apologies for my mistakes. It has helped. I was a disappointment like the fathers before me. Now it is my turn to right the wrong. We have an obligation to our kids no matter what the situation is men. It's not easy dealing with my sons and their moms. I've prayed for over 10 years to see relationships restored. Anything is possible for us with God's help. My hope is in Him alone, not in man or myself. Be a father or at least try. You might get a miracle. God can open any door.

Chapter 39 - When Love Comes to Town
Rick

It's okay to start slow. I can talk about Jesus all day long but until you meet Him face-to-face you're not gonna understand Him like I understand Him. Not that I'm better than you, but I have a different experience of God than you do. Everyone does! God is good! I know this and He wants to do good things in my life. We tend to mess it up. He wants to do crazy cool things. If it starts to be about my effort to make something happen, it's finished. It's a lot more fun the way God does it. He has a love for us that is deep and supreme. He will make a way for us, even when there is no way.

We had a stirring in our hearts to adopt another kid. Our age was a factor in our thoughts about the whole thing. We wanted to be smart, but that familiar urging would not go away. Having kids graduating high school in your late 50s or 60s is a challenge for any parent. We went to visit the county again and started the process. Our Samuel was about six years old. We knew it was the right thing. We were qualified quickly. It was challenging, but not as much as previous attempts were. So we started getting phone calls about potential kids that were available. We would pray about each one, but none of them felt right. They called five times and we said no five times. It was weird, but it was the right thing. Then came the call. It was a Monday morning. We were called about a little boy, seven weeks old. We prayed and the Lord filled the room so fully that we said, "Let's go pick up our son." We got Samuel out of school and picked up a few things we needed like formula and diapers. We had been open to any age under six, but we didn't have what we needed for an infant any longer at home.

He was seven weeks old. We picked him up and he looked a little pale. The caseworker said to take him to the hospital. He was sick. We went to the closest one and as soon as they saw him, the whole staff went into motion. The nurses swarmed him and they admitted him instantly. It was early March and it turned out he had pneumonia and the flu. One nurse said they had four infants die from that the previous month in Colorado. I was pissed she was speaking death over my son. I said, "We'll see." They said he would need oxygen and he would be in the hospital for two weeks. I said, "We'll see."

They started doing every test they could think of. They even did a spinal tap. After five hours I told my wife to go home and take Samuel with her. "I'll take the night shift," I said. It was a long day. I went to eat in the cafeteria. This little boy was finally in a room, with tubes and machines hooked up to him. The staff understood when I wanted to stay the night and be with him. I was dozing off about 9:30 when I smelled something I had never smelled before. It was like death with a kerosene gravy. I woke up quickly. I couldn't see or hear them, but a horde of demonic entities had entered the room. This was new! I could perceive their malice and the smell was awful. I stood up, and said with a level of confidence and power I didn't know I had, "I don't know who you are and what you think you can do here, but that's my son and if you want to throw down, then let's throw down."

And we did. I was speaking scripture and blessing over my son, breaking off generational curses and dismantling a demonic platoon in the process. It was a battle all night long! I was committed to his freedom and nothing would deter me. My wife showed up in the morning so I could shower and get some sleep, and I came back the next night for another night shift. Guess who showed up again? It was the same bunch as the night before, same smell, different day. Only this time they came in wounded, beaten up and hobbling. I heard the Lord laughing behind me. There is nothing like that feeling. God is laughing at your enemies! He wants to fight with you and defeat them together! The demons just dropped their heads and walked out quietly. They were already defeated. Something changed in me at that moment. The Lord and I had a blast that night exploring all the blessings for my son. I spoke life over him in every realm and in each place where his body needed healing. The next day we took him home from the hospital. He had no flu symptoms, no pneumonia and his color returned to him. I was so excited for that little man. He got freedom that only God can give because his daddy knew who he was and who God is. It was more powerful than I realized, and Luke has come so far.

Every child is precious. Can you imagine what a difference we can make if we men will rise up for our kids and make a stand for them? Get busy men, someone stood up for you once, or maybe they didn't. Now it's your turn. Remember, even if you had no daddy, you have a Father in heaven who loves you and was working on your behalf even if you never knew or realized it. And He is right now! He will do the same for your children, but He would prefer if you partner with him. Make a difference today! You may be the only one who stands up for the little children. God rewards those who look out for the orphans and the widows. It's a joyful thing. The kids I have worked with, many of them have horrific stories. All of them special and needed a little help along the way. We all need that! The fullness of life that comes as we help others will bring healing in our souls and blessing to the hearts of minds of the next generation. That's a legacy we can all leave behind! And we should.

Chapter 40 - Honor Your Father and Mother

Exodus 20:12 Honor your father and mother, that it may go well with you (your days be prolonged) in the land which the Lord your God gives you.

Read Psalm 90.

God uses the good ones and the bad ones. Some try and use God for their own purposes. Who do you want to be? We have taken extra care to be as honest as possible about what happened to us. With all that we've said and shared, it may seem that we hate our parents and have nothing to do with them. That's not the point at all. At some level we love our parents, but we don't love what happened to us. They made choices and did what they did. It's not wrong to tell the truth. Our desire is not to embarrass them or make them poster children for poor parenting. The point is, everyone is human with struggles, issues and problems. All of us have the capability of being insanely evil and incredibly compassionate. It all depends on how we deal with life, what we focus on and how we forgive. There will always be a need for forgiveness. We highly recommend it. It breaks off chains, sadness and fears and it can set others free as well. Anyone can do it, but it is a choice to make. You alone must choose. Forgiving someone does not mean that you have to see them. You have to set good boundaries and be safe. Forgiveness can be done after someone has died, or moved away. It doesn't have to be in person. It doesn't have to be out loud. Do what keeps you safe and secure. Don't allow an old abuser to get into your life again. Don't spend time with toxic people who steal your joy, create drama or make you sad. It is your life. Live it in a way that nurtures and encourages you. Life is too short for drama and victimhood. If you need to get out of a situation, please do. Get help if you need to. If you still can't get free, we have included email addresses you can contact us to help you. We want to see you get free. Let's get over our stuff. Yes it's hard work. Yes it sucks to go back to the muck and dig it all up again. We did that to write this book and it's not easy or fun. Getting free never is. The reward will be worth it. You have what it takes already inside of you. You can do it and you will. So walk into freedom and fill your heart with joy. I guarantee the process will not always be smooth and simple, but if you go through it to the end here's what will happen:

1. You will be free of the junk in your life.
2. You will find peace beyond understanding.
3. You will make changes that help everyone around you.
4. You will see purpose in your suffering.
5. You will become a lighthouse to help others.
6. You will find strength and wisdom you didn't know was there.
7. You will change the world for better.

Are we God's TV set? Did He create us just to have something to do? Did He wind us up just to see what we would do with it all? That's what a lot of people think. He's far off, He doesn't care they say. Maybe we used to think that, too. When He reveals Himself to you in a way that there is no other explanation, then you'll know He is real and that He is good! He intervenes at just the right moment. If we don't want Him, He will respect our choice, even letting us go to hell if that's what we want. He's a gentleman. He does love us and He does want to be with us. His heart is to love His children and He's really good at it. Let Him love you. Please.

Go forward. Take care of your health: physical, emotional and spiritual. Live to the future, not from the past. Be a light to others, so they can find their way. That's our hope and desire in writing this book. To encourage you to make your life into something beautiful. No matter what has happened, you can be different, you can overcome; you will succeed if you try and if you believe it! The words you say can have a big impact, too. Learn to speak life over yourself, not curses or judgment. The tongue is powerful. Resolve to be someone else if you need to and then act according to that new persona. Usually a person has to change about every four to five years to keep up with all they are learning. How's it going? Do you need some updating? I know we do, that's why we wrote this book. After all these years, it was time.

Forgiveness is extremely powerful and if you have the opportunity to forgive someone, welcome to the human race! We all will sometime. If, like us, you have been given an incredibly challenging scenario to overcome and to forgive, congratulations. If you are chosen to forgive, it is a privilege. It really is. It may not feel like it, but you get more wisdom, more compassion and more opportunity for growth! Keep up the good work, be the amazing person that you are and please let us know if we can help you! Jesus was chosen to forgive the whole world by His blood. If you've been chosen to forgive, too, you're in good company! God bless you all! It's an honor to serve you, please let us know how we can help you. Our e-mail address is listed below. If you would like some free samples from "I'll Be Your Father" a new book by Rick coming out in 2017, feel free to contact us anytime! Have a great life, you are special and one of a kind! God wants the best for you and we do, too! Let's all be good ambassadors for God and to each other. We're all in this life together, be a friend, be a neighbor, be the good news that someone needs to hear. Please share with us how this book has challenged, helped or made sense to you. We want to see you come fully into your destiny, it's why we're here! It may help us understand something in a new way or open up ideas and ways to help even more people. Let us know how we can help you, answer your questions, but also how we can celebrate you!

The secret of change is to focus all of your energy, not on fighting the old, but on building the new.
-Socrates

Love and blessings be upon you!

Marcus and Rick
July 20, 2016
chosentoforgive@gmail.com

Chapter 41 - Exercises That Help the Process

Rick's next book called, "I'll Be Your Father," will be published soon. There are many excerpts from that book as well as some helpful exercises to help you process your life. We're trying to develop leaders, not surround ourselves with followers. Everyone can be a leader but it usually takes a process to get there. That process can be difficult and stressful, but if you surround yourself with positive, mature, loving, and competent people who will help you, it will be a lot easier. Clarity, understanding, and purpose are the desired outcomes and remember, not every leader will be liked by everybody. A thicker skin is a useful tool, and so is integrity. Empathy, patience, and courtesy are all a plus, too, as well as healthy relationships, both physically and emotionally.

It is okay not to get it perfect the first time, you can't be wrong when you're still learning! Don't fix the symptoms, go to the root issues and work on those. That's where lasting change can happen. Confront the struggle and work through it. Either you're the one driving the car or you're the car and something, or someone, is driving you. Transformation is evident when you embrace a different way of doing life than before. Hopefully our stories have helped you remember who you are, engaged with you and shared some ideas to ponder. The sky is the limit! Set your sights on the highest place and have fun getting there! This process can be deep water, take your time, it's not a test, but a tool to use. Be true to yourself. Check and see where you are, see if this helps you gain understanding. Feel free to share what you learn with us and others it's what we live for! Here's to commitments that last. Enjoy!

Chapter 42 - A New Way of Thinking

Circumstances are a tool to reveal our identity; they are not what defines our identity. If things are going poorly or in a challenging way, there is purpose in it. It is meant to reveal parts of you that are incomplete or missing, not to highlight failures and faults. It is always to build you up, not to tear you down or make you feel small. God is different in how he acts toward us than anyone else is. When we receive Jesus we get a total transformation package. We get forgiveness for sin but so much more. We get the entire Kingdom of God given to us with all the resources and provisions of it in Jesus from the beginning. That doesn't mean that all of it is activated from the start. God is wise enough to help us learn how to use the gifts and power of His kingdom in responsible ways. He wants to show us how it works. It's always going to be for His glory and for our best. He works in wisdom, not logic. He can redeem time to get us back on schedule if we're running behind where we should be. He initiates and we respond. All His answers are yes and amen, until He tells us to wait or stop. The possibilities are endless, but His timing is perfect. We have to learn to work with Him if we want His perfection to show up! It's not rules, regulations or performance that matter, that's religion. The key is knowing God personally and doing the right things with joy. That's the Kingdom of God, it's not more you have to do to be accepted. It's understanding you are already accepted in the Beloved (Jesus). The Father loves everything about you, every wart and all. He is committed to you and He will never leave you nor forsake you. It's good, very good, to be in His loving gaze. He will make a way for you and me where there is no way!

We are not ordinary or mediocre. We need to teach our kids about Jesus. We have done a poor job of that. We also need to let the Holy Spirit teach us. We have also done a poor job of letting Him. We have the favor of God on us so we should set our minds on things above. Tests are allowed to let us see where we are in the process of growing up. There is an old you which is passing away and a new you which is coming forth. We can't fix the old man, it is crucified with Christ. It is dead. Instead we have to focus on the new man that we're becoming and make every effort to activate new ways of thinking, seeing and speaking to be more like Jesus. It's not just seeing differently, it's a whole new thought altogether. It's working on the positive until it's fully established, not trying to fix what is wrong. We have to take possession of ourselves and win the fight on the inside to be made new in a way that will last. We must be unstoppable in this pursuit. We must keep the ground or territory we have been given by God or agree with the lie the enemy is telling us and forfeit our promised land to him. Our process is something like this: we get a realization of a need or an area of lack within our lives, then we go through training to become more like Christ, overcome the flesh or the past and then we are tested on it to prove that we are this new person that we're trying to become. The gift is given, we just have to learn how to use it. The only way we can do that is to engage with God, learn and grow, and do it His way. That's true in every area of our lives. The old has passed away and the new has come. How are you doing with that?

2 Corinthians 5:17
Therefore if anyone is in Christ, he is a new creation; the old things passed away; behold, new things have come.
Luke 19:1-10
1 He (Jesus) entered Jericho and was passing through. 2 And there was a man called by the name of Zaccheus; he was a chief tax collector and he was rich. 3 Zaccheus was trying to see who Jesus was, and was unable because of the crowd, for he was small in stature. 4 So he ran on ahead and climbed up into a sycamore tree in order to see Him, for He was about to pass through that way. 5 When Jesus came to the place, He looked up and said to him, "Zaccheus, hurry and come down, for today I must stay at your house." 6 And he hurried and came down and received Him (Jesus) gladly. 7 When they saw it, they all began to grumble, saying, "He has gone to be the guest of a man who is a sinner." 8 Zaccheus stopped and said to the Lord, "Behold, Lord, half of my possessions I will give to the poor, and if I have defrauded anyone of anything, I will give back four times as much." 9 And Jesus said to him,

"Today salvation has come to this house, because he, too, is a son of Abraham. 10 For the Son of Man has come to seek and to save that which was lost."

Trauma turns into transformation with Jesus. Zaccheus was the most hated man in his town, but when Jesus invited Z to host Him for lunch, it made him the most honored man in town. Zaccheus' response was to change from his previous behavior and make up for his poor choices of the past. So when he got the affirming message from Jesus, the whole town was different afterwards and the change was everywhere. It was prosperity, restoration and transformation. The law required any theft to be paid back in full at four times the amount of what was stolen. When the restoration came to the town, it was like everyone won the lottery. Jesus changed one heart but hundreds, maybe thousands of people benefitted from that change inside one guy. That's how it's supposed to be. One changed heart changes thousands. That can be you and me. We have a chance to make a difference in the lives of everyone we meet. When we bring restoration to others it can change cities. Instead of protesting the wrongs, why don't we bring honor to those who don't appear to deserve honor. Let's believe that God is active in the affairs of men and is able to change our course if we will operate the way He does.

It made absolutely no sense for Jesus to give honor to a thief. The tax collectors would charge the required taxes on behalf of the Roman Empire and overcharge as much as they wanted to get exceedingly rich. The Romans just wanted their cut to build and maintain the empire. The tax collectors were viewed as traitors for ripping off their own people, for getting rich on the backs of others and agreeing with the Roman tyranny of taxation and oppression. They were the most hated people in all Israel. Zaccheus saw his choices were wrong, but he didn't just confess them, he restored all that was stolen including the penalty that was required. Imagine a knock on the door and upon opening it, here's the most hated person you know. Your first instinct is to cut his throat, but he speaks and says, "I'm sorry, I stole this money from you over a long time and now I'm giving it back with the required

223

penalty of four times more. Here you go." You stand there stunned as he hands you a bag filled with gold coins and it's more money than you've ever seen before. Suddenly your world has changed forever, the treason you endured, the struggle, oppression and poverty are all washed away in a moment. That is transformation! No longer are you carefully budgeting so you can eat, you're starting businesses, investing in the future and having a party to celebrate.

Zaccheus was a totally changed man, and when he was, the whole town was changed, too. How would your town look with no more racism, no more lack of what we need, no more fear of the future? What could your world look like if Jesus paid your town a visit? Maybe like me, Jesus is coming to visit you, not to tell me what I'm doing wrong, but to affirm me and tell me He loves me. He wants to be with me and help me understand how to do this life. There is perfection and peace in what He is offering and I want to say yes. Religion says you have to do this list of things to be accepted. Jesus says, "I accept you just the way you are!" Notice He didn't tell Z all the things he had to do to make up for the sins and mistakes. No, Jesus says, "I must have lunch with you!" He affirms him in front of everyone. I'm sure most of them were pissed! Traveling teachers (Rabbis) were hosted by families in the towns they came to, usually a wealthy or righteous family was given the honor. Here, it's the worst slime ball ever!

Jesus is so funny and doesn't do things the way we would. That invitation changed the whole town. Who can we interact with to change the whole town for the better? We can do a great work of restoration by choosing to help someone who is awful by choosing to see the good in them, so they can, too! People get a little off track at times, but they are still special to God. They have value, they are created with a plan and a purpose as we are. If we forget that, we might miss a chance to help them and maybe change our whole town in the process. A lot of people need correction, but most don't need to be reminded of their failures. They already know. They need to be loved. Remember love conquers all, and if we want to win, that is our greatest tool and blessing to share. Love. Take it out for a spin. Many of the political movements you see now only focus on the negative. That is not God's way. It makes no sense to build up accusations when affirmations do a much better job of changing someone! God would rather call up your goodness than put down your weakness. We need to learn this part, too!

Joshua 24:15 But if serving the Lord seems undesirable to you, then choose for yourselves this day whom you will serve, whether the gods your ancestors served beyond the Euphrates, or the gods of the Amorites, in whose land you are living. But as for me and my household, we will serve the Lord."

Chapter 43 - Deeper Water

God knows who you are. That's a really good thing, because He loves us completely even though He knows us intimately. These verses are a huge encouragement because we are not ordinary, so-so or mediocre. We are purposeful, important, valuable and significant. We are seen and treasured, we are loved and cared for. More than we ever realized. Read on to see how God sees you and has cared for you since before you existed.

Read Psalm 139 and Romans 8
This is who we are. It's a good thing to learn, to believe and make it a part of you at every level. God is good and He wants the best for us. Let's rejoice and be glad in that and then treat others the same way. If we focus on the good, we will bring forth good. If we focus on the garbage we will bring that forth. Thanks for taking this journey with us:

<u>We bless you:</u>
We ask the Father to fill your heart and mind with peace
We thank Him that you are a beloved child, filled with life and wonder
We bless your relationships, businesses, families, dreams, plans and purposes
We ask for a powerful expression of love to you from Our Father
We bless you with creativity, laughter, joy and hope beyond understanding
We call forward all the special blessings, calling, gifts and talents in your life, may they be significant
to build up your hope and faith and to be a delight, a help and a benefit to everyone you meet.

Numbers 6:24-26

Now may the Lord bless you and keep you, make His face shine on you and be gracious to you, look upon you with favor and give you peace. Amen!

Chapter 44 – Epilogue

Sometimes it seems like, you can't choose to forgive and you have to be chosen to forgive. Unforgiveness is a high cost no one can pay. The most important thing in this book is the concept, the act of forgiveness. Whatever has happened and whatever we have said about people in this book, please hear this: We want to forgive what has happened to us first and foremost. We can forgive and we are choosing to do that. You can, too! You have the same choice to forgive others as well. This blueprint will help you do just that.

Forgiveness is powerful. You'll feel your power when you say this out loud alone or with others:

We grant forgiveness to anyone who has used, neglected, sexually abused, poisoned, ignored or physically abused us including our parents, relatives, neighbors, friends, drug dealers, teachers, coaches, co-workers, employers, supervisors, babysitters, the government, media people, educational people or systems, religious leaders, artists, entertainers, police officers, social services workers and anyone else.

We ask God for forgiveness for all the politicians who have lied to us, used us, abused us, wasted our money or resources, or sold us down the river. This includes all of our U.S. Presidents: Barack Obama, Bill Clinton, both George Bushes, Ronald Reagan, Jimmy Carter, Gerald Ford, Richard Nixon, Lyndon B. Johnson, John F. Kennedy, Dwight D. Eisenhower, Harry S. Truman, Franklin D. Roosevelt, Herbert Hoover, Calvin Coolidge, Warren Harding, Woodrow Wilson, William Howard Taft, Theodore Roosevelt, William McKinley, Grover Cleveland, Benjamin Harrison, Chester A. Arthur, James A. Garfield, Rutherford B. Hayes, Ulysses S. Grant, Andrew Johnson, Abraham Lincoln, James Buchanan, Franklin Pierce, Millard Fillmore, Zachary Taylor, James Polk, John Tyler, William Henry Harrison, Martin Van Buren, Andrew Jackson, John Quincy Adams, James Monroe, James Madison, Thomas Jefferson, John Adams and George Washington for whatever they did wrong willingly or unwillingly to hurt America, our heritage or any people of any nation past, present or future.

We ask forgiveness for every Vice President, every cabinet member, each and every member of the US Senate and The House of Representatives for any wrongs committed on their watch under all those U.S. Presidents.

We ask forgiveness for all the judges at every level including the Supreme Court who have ever served America in any capacity and acted wrongly, took advantage of others or interpreted the law with wrong motives.

We ask forgiveness for everyone who ever served our country in any branch of the military, active or reserves and took advantage of, killed or mistreated other people groups, women or civilians.

We ask forgiveness for any spiritual or religious leaders who have lied to us, stolen from us, hindered us, tainted the truth, acted arrogantly, forgot who God is, taught people poorly or inaccurately and loved money or the spotlight more than God or their people.

We ask forgiveness for the media people and companies for every time they told us a lie, tainted or ignored the truth, misled us, used us for unknown purposes, made us less than we are, had their own agenda, invited corruption or valued money above us.

We ask forgiveness for any government workers who have been corrupt, acted arrogantly, selfishly or been lazy.

We ask forgiveness for anyone in the education system who lead us astray from the truth, taught us perversion, took advantage of us, promoted lies, mistreated us, poisoned us or was prejudice against us.

We ask forgiveness for anyone in the entertainment industry including the arts, books, movies, magazines, music, cable or network TV shows who corrupted our morals, taught us lies, modeled rebellion, made lewd things seem acceptable, promoted perversion and violence or used us for their money making schemes.

We ask forgiveness for our doctors and hospitals for making mistakes, charging too much, promoting pharmaceuticals as a first option, taking kickbacks, taking advantage of our lack of knowledge, putting us at risk, for consenting to do abortions, loving money and not caring deeply for us or our futures.

We ask forgiveness for police, firemen, social workers and other first responders for not helping us, protecting us, serving us or seeing us as valuable.

We ask forgiveness for any corporations, business people or others who put us at risk by selling us dangerous products, poor quality items, or misleading us just to take our money.

We ask forgiveness for everyone who took advantage of us willingly or unwillingly; to everyone who tried to keep us down, manipulated us, told lies about us, cursed us, partnered with evil entities or people, hated us, stole our dreams or money,and anything else that was done against us, willingly or unwillingly.

We ask forgiveness for all the world systems and crime that have come against us including communism, abortion, radical religion, fascism, religious systems, dictatorships, Nazis, skin heads, gangsters, outlaws, rapists, evil, hatefulness, bigotry, manipulative, liars, thieves, arrogant, greedy, sexually impure, drug warlords, aristocracy, exploitation, slavery, shedding innocent blood, taking advantage of others, false witnessing, wicked plans, witchcraft, racism and hatred.

We ask forgiveness for the poor treatment of Native Americans who were murdered, lied to, rounded up, had their land stolen, were not honored in treaties, threatened and taken advantage of in so many ways.

We ask God for forgiveness for Hillary Clinton, for being corrupt, for stealing our future, lying, judgements, promoting disunity, putting America at risk, cultivating radical views and being incomplete. We ask God to help her, save her and give her the fullness of life that only God can give and help her repent from her ways to serve God and His plans and purposes for America.

We ask God for forgiveness for Donald Trump, for being rude, loud, prideful, obnoxious and arrogant. We ask forgiveness for insults, judgements, uncertainty, wrong attitudes towards women and minorities, being incomplete and for the ability to insult people. We ask God to help him, save him and give him the fullness of life that only God can give and help him repent from his ways to serve God and His plans and purposes for America.

We ask forgiveness for us and our fellow Americans for believing the lies, being apathetic, not helping each other, allowing disunity to take hold, hurting each other, finding faults, speaking harshly, promoting anarchy, having abortions, complaining, misusing people, resources and things, not speaking the truth, killing each other, being hypocrites, defaulting to negatives, complaining and whining.

We grant forgiveness to God for all the times we suffered, felt pain, felt alone, spoke in anger, hated you and wondered if you really loved us. We didn't know who you really were and we are sorry for doubting you. Please forgive us for our wrong view of your loving and gentle spirit. You are a good Father!

We grant forgiveness to ourselves for not learning, growing up at the wrong pace, not making good choices, doing crime, wasting time, for not believing God, having sex wrongly, using drugs, alcohol or pornography, for forgetting who we are, believing the lies and for taking so long to do what we're made for. Also for anything we might have overlooked or forgotten to forgive ourselves for.

We ask for a new spirit of unity and love to rise up and fill all Americans today!

We ask for recompense for all that's been stolen from us, delayed, hindered, misplaced, given away, left behind, manipulated away and hidden.

We are the United States of America. A nation united can never fall. A nation divided can be defeated. We can no longer allow ourselves to be divided by those who hate us or our way of life. We must ignore the negativity of the media and seek to reconcile ourselves with others. There is something at work trying to destroy us from the inside. Let's resist it and make peace with each other. America is great, there is nowhere else like it, ever, in history of the planet. It was, and is a gift from God Himself, through faithful men and women who conceived a nation based on law and a spirit of goodness. Let's return to that while there is still time. We are black and white, red and yellow, we are male and female, we are gay and straight, we are tall and short, we agree and we don't, and that's okay. We're all in this together and we have a lot more in common than we know. Let's be about making friends and helping others as much as we can. Mentors are needed, ambassadors, bridge builders and so much more. Let's work together. America needs to be united! It's built to last, so let's protect it! Love your neighbor, meet a new friend and reconcile with someone. It's time to be great people again! We have a toxic culture and media filled with hatred and animosity, we have a hateful countenance and what we need are a new generation of founding fathers to guide us back from the edge, away from the abyss!

We are so excited for where things are going. We have a 501c3 that was approved on July 20, 2016 called Legacy Grace Community Development Corporation. It has a mission focus on affordable housing and economic development, including business start-ups like the Miracle Street Gallery art gallery and more. We are looking at buildings, raising money and working hard to change lives, restore dignity to others and make a prosperous way for everyone we meet. We have spent the past twenty years learning what works and what doesn't in all facets of mentoring and working with various people who are homeless, ex-offenders, disabled, low income, underappreciated and forgotten. That was us before and now we can help others to overcome. You can, too! The process is supposed to work that way. Get past your circumstances and use it as springboard to help someone else in the same situation to succeed.

We have a training program for leaders, game changers, administrators and champions. Your community needs you and me to be awesome, amazing and purposeful in all we do. There is no place like it to draw people into a new way of thinking, doing and being. We needed help along the way. We still do. If we can help you, please let us know. We are committed to your success and your wonderful future. If you would like to know more about what we're doing please contact us as listed below. The past is not always a gift, but it is preparation for all that you are becoming. It has purpose and value. If you were chosen to forgive like we were, we salute you! It's important to find out who you

233

are and to become who you are supposed to be. There is only one you and the world needs you. Your destiny is calling, answer it and say yes and join us on this excellent adventure. You'll never be bored!

Have a great day, every day! It's all before you, you can do it! It's already inside you! We can help! If you would like to participate in affordable housing, economic development, restoration for low income, ex-offenders or homeless please contact us as listed below. Donations are tax deductible. We're hoping to raise $7 million this year for three projects. One is a live and work farm, another is an apartment building and the third is a group home for the homeless and low income to help them change their financial situation. Many of them have amazing talent and just need a little help to get started. We may use crowdfunding to help us, too! So many possibilities! We would love your help!

For more information about training, speaking engagements, workshops, to buy products or to donate to the many causes of restoring freedom, please contact us at the locations listed below:

website	www.chosentoforgive.com
phone	720-774-4677
email	chosentoforgive@gmail.com